THE ETHICAL WRITER'S GUIDE TO HARNESSING THE POWER OF AI

USING AI WITH INTEGRITY

H. J. PHILLIPS

CONTENTS

FOREWORD

GEORGINA DEAN

You've heard that artificial intelligence is the 'hot' new thing on the market, saving people a slew of time at work, and you're wondering if it can do the same thing for your writing? Maybe you find yourself on the other side of the fence, and you're worried that AI is going to replace you as an author? Well, whether you believe that AI's the answer to skyrocketing your career, or whether you believe your tradecraft is at risk of becoming obsolete, you have definitely picked-up the right book!

I first met HJ and her family during our adventures working overseas, a connection which first began as colleagues, and since transpired into lifelong friendship. We worked together at a K-12 International School, where I was supporting digital strategy as the Director of Learning Technology at that time.

One morning I received a message from HJ telling me she had something exciting to share with me. I waited with eager anticipation to connect with her over Zoom later that day. "AI, Georgina, I'm going to write a book to help writers with AI! Where can I start?" she asked. I was overwhelmed with joy and excited for this project, such a time-relevant piece that would positively impact all those in her industry.

Fast forwarding a few months, I wasn't surprised to read the incredible depths she'd since taken, to explore a wide range of high-quality AI tools that could meaningfully and purposefully be used to support the writing industry.

Although AI has been around for a long time now, it has really taken a monumental turn since November 2022, leaving many feeling overwhelmed in their respective sectors. I can only imagine how those in the writing industry may feel, with the gloom-and-doom of autonomous writing breaking headlines, and possibly leaving authors panicking about the future of their careers. But please rest assured, this book will easily calm these worries in the following chapters, using her creative expertise as an author and curiosity in pushing the boundaries of that tradecraft.

Will this book then, give you all kinds of secrets about how AI can write for you? Well, yes and no, to be exact. This book is definitely going to help you maximise the time you invest into each of your writing stages: planning, writing, editing, and publishing, as it equally highlights all the reasons why it cannot replace you as a writer. She's demonstrated a very impressive balance of ways in which AI can benefit the writing process, whilst highlighting the pitfalls which we all need to be mindful of.

Even though this book will be extremely beneficial for authors during any stage of their career, I especially recommend this as a must-read for any new and upcoming author, as the writing method is seamlessly simplified into digestible and actionable workflows.

Remember...in a world fully accessible, modifiable, and overflowing with data, it's more important now than ever before, to verify everything that we hear, watch, and read. The pages that you are about to consume will equip you with key strategies to help you do just this! As you embark on this next part of your authoring journey, taking your first guided steps into writing with AI, don't forget your post-its, digital word doc, highlighters, and/or bullet-journal as you go - you won't want to miss out on any of the gems HJ shares with you.

I look forward to reading about how this book has either inspired your risk-taking with AI writing tools, reassured your qualms about life-as-an-author in the 'age of AI', or even improved the quality of your work by using these new digital writing techniques.

Georgina Dean isa certified Product Manager, a CSPO, an ISTE Certified Educator, a Google for Education Certified Trainer & Innovator (#VIA20), an Adobe Education Leader, a Microsoft Innovative Educator, and an Apple Teacher, with a goal to support communities with sustainable digital transformation roadmaps and innovative product solutions. Also, as a visionary leader, mentor, coach, writer, livestreamer, and keynote speaker, she is keen to impact creative innovation across EMEA, where she has been fostering impactful change across education for over a decade. She empowers others with the strategies and creative confidence they need to be successful members of a global community.

INTRODUCTION

Stop. Before you delve deeper into the pages of the book, I want to make sure it's the right book for you. If you are looking for a get-rich-quick guide that will show you how to use AI (artificial intelligence) technology to generate a book in a day, then sorry but you are in the wrong place.

But neither is this book going to demonise AI tech and prophesy doom and gloom for the future of writing.

This is a book designed to help you understand the implications and applications of AI to your writing career. To show those of you in the creative field that are scared, why you don't need to be. And why those of you who think you will just be able to AI to write a book for you and make millions are currently rather delusional.

The Ethical Writer's Guide to Harnessing the Power of AI does exactly what it says on the tin. Come with me and learn how you can utilise AI to support your creative process, helping your write better and faster.

In today's world, we are becoming more and more familiar with the concept of AI, and what was once a subject only for science fiction is now a part of our everyday life – whether we see it or not. Obviously there is huge controversy around the use of AI; there always is with revolutionary advancements. I am not going to use this book as a platform to argue the rights and wrongs of AI, the fact is, it is here.

Now, I can say, hand on heart, that with all my love for AI technology and how frequently I turn to it for support, I have never copied a single sentence from software and used it in my writing. (I wrote my first 25 fiction books before it even existed.) And yet, despite this, I still think it is the most invaluable tool I have discovered in the last ten years . So please, sit down with a cup of tea or beverage of choice, and settle in while we begin this journey. (Actually, you might want to be near a computer so you can start playing around with some of these tools as you go.) I will show you real-life situations and places where I have used AI to guide my writing, not write for me. Primarily this book is aimed at fiction writers, but there will hopefully still be plenty of useful information for non-fiction writers too.

Given the title of the book, it's important that I mention ethics early on. I have two golden rules that I follow:

1) Don't ask AI to write for you.

As I go through the book, you will see that I never ask any of the AI programmes to write original content for direct use in my novels. Never copy verbatim anything AI generates for you into your book and attempt to pass it off as your own work. (It is also suggested that you give credit to the AI for any ideas or content that it provides you with.)

2) Don't use existing author's names in your prompts.

Never invoke the names of other authors by asking AI it to write in the style of another author or mimic their work. This would put you at risk of copyright infringement and mean you could face legal consequences.

And if you don't want to believe me, see what ChatGPT says about it. ChatGPT response.

Fig 0.1

What ethical implications do I need to consider when using AI to help write a novel?

When using AI to help write a novel, there are several ethical implications to consider. Here are some important considerations:

1. Intellectual property: Ensure that the AI system you use does not infringe upon the intellectual property rights of others. It should not be trained on copyrighted materials or generate content that directly copies existing works without appropriate modifications. Respect the rights of authors and creators.
2. Attribution and authorship: Clearly indicate the contributions made by the AI system in your novel. Take responsibility for the parts that were generated by AI and give appropriate credit to the system or technology used. Be transparent with readers about the involvement of AI in the creative process.

3. Misrepresentation and deception: Avoid using AI-generated content in a way that may deceive or mislead readers. If the AI system generates content that imitates a particular writing style or voice, clearly disclose that it is the work of AI and not a human author. Misrepresentation could erode trust and raise ethical concerns.
4. Bias and fairness: AI systems can inherit biases present in the data they are trained on. Be cautious of any biases that may be present in the AI-generated content and strive to address them. Ensure that your novel promotes diversity, inclusivity, and fairness, and consider using AI as a tool to enhance these aspects rather than perpetuate biases.
5. Privacy and data protection: When using an AI system, be mindful of the data you provide to train or fine-tune it. Respect privacy rights and ensure that any personal or sensitive information is appropriately handled and protected.
6. Unintended consequences: AI systems may generate unexpected or unintended content. Review and evaluate the AI-generated content carefully to ensure it aligns with your ethical standards and the intended purpose of your novel.

It is essential to approach the use of AI in novel writing with ethical awareness, ensuring transparency, accountability, and responsible use of technology.

As you can clearly see, AI programmes (or them programmers) have no desire to take over from real people. Which leads me on to another brief point.

Why I don't think AI will be writing full-length novels any time soon.

I'm going to keep this it very brief because it doesn't fit in with the aim of the book, which is to teach you how to use AI to develop your writing. I am also hoping it will alleviate some people's worries that they will wake up tomorrow and no longer have a profession, because the dreaded AI has replaced them. I will also circle back to this at the end, to shine a light on a couple of issues that we will have raised along the way, and hopefully to offer you a little more assurance.

When I was young, my brother and I learned to play the piano. I only learned because I wanted to do everything my brother could do, but it turned out I rather liked it. So much so that I went on and studied music. When it became clear to my parents that playing the piano was more than a passing fad for me, they got me a keyboard. A large, 88 keys, Casio something or other, with lights that flashed and hundreds of in-built songs. In-built songs, that I listened to with delight when I first received the gift, then forgot entirely about as I went on learning to be a better player. The thing is, those songs, while played note perfectly, were simply digital sounds, played in the same order and the same rhythms as famous pieces of music. I did not listen to them and appreciate the skill that went into composing a piece like that. I did not play them on repeat, hoping to one day sound like them. They were flat, digital reflections, and I wanted music.

The point of a story, be it a piece of flash fiction or a novel, serves the same purpose as a piece of music; to evoke emotion. It doesn't matter what the genre is; as a writer, composer, or performer you want your audience to feel something. As a novelist that might be the rush of adrenaline as your heroine escapes a deadly situation, or the weepy heartbreak of a lost love that causes the reader to cry into the pages. Stories are focused on emotion. Another key factor in a great story is tension. Be that the tension that we all feel waiting for our protagonists' first kiss, or during the mistreatment of one of our favourite characters. A captivating novel is full of tension. And while AI can describe the physical effects of emotions and when said emotions are most frequently felt, they do not have the ability to actually feel them. They do not understand tension's burgeoning effects on a person, or feel the physical responses to a flood of relief when a character has been saved. Because of that, they cannot understand, beyond a programmed level, the importance of beats and flow and pauses in action. They would never see how emotions could drive a character to behave responsibly or irrationally. They can merely extrapolate from the information they have been given. Use patterns to predict a likely outcome. AI does not have, for want of a better word, the humanity that is required to create a beautiful piece of prose. And until that is developed, we don't need to worry.

One last thing before we start

Due to the nature of software developments and changing regulations, I am aware that some of the information might quickly become outdated. If you sign up with the QR code you will automatically receive notifications anytime I update a chapter. In addition, you will then receive the updated chapter FREE. In this fashion I hope this book will continue to be relevant for as long as possible.

Now let's look at how writers can use AI, and in particularly ChatGPT to elevate and streamline our writing as novelists.

1. THE ONLY THESAURUS YOU'LL EVER NEED?

I UNDERSTAND THAT STARTING WITH A THESAURUS MIGHT SEEM SMALL. Let's be honest, you've purchased a book about the most powerful piece of computer software ever developed, and I begin by discussing something that has been around for over 150 years. A thesaurus is a tool that you can carry around in book form or easily search on your computer. After all, internet searches are sufficient for sourcing words, aren't they? Well, to be honest, not anymore. Since using ChatGPT as a thesaurus, I very rarely return to my previously long-trusted internet search pages.

I know there might be some of you out there who believe that you shouldn't need to use a thesaurus, that you should already know all the words you want to use. However, you obviously don't suffer with that issue that many of us do, where we know there's a better word, and we've used it often enough, but our brain just can't remember what that word is. A problem that is definitely getting worse as I get older.

So, why is ChatGPT better than a standard thesaurus? To start with, it can be summarised in one word: **context**. When you ask ChatGPT to search for synonyms, you can search for them within a sentence, thereby providing the context you need. How many times have you looked up a word online, such as "match" or "set," and had to scroll through various nouns and verbs with the same meaning until you found what you wanted? That inconvenience is a thing of the past.

Fig 1.1

Good afternoon. Please can you give me synonyms for the word "fine," in the context of a fine pencil?

Good afternoon! In the context of a fine pencil, "fine" refers to the thinness or precision of the pencil tip. Here are some synonyms for "fine" in this context:

1. Thin
2. Slim
3. Narrow
4. Delicate
5. Precise
6. Sharp
7. Fine-point
8. Fine-tipped

Please note that some of these synonyms may be more suitable depending on the specific context in which you're using the term.

It knows the meaning of the word I want to convey, so it only gives my synonyms that match with that.

We can take this even further. For me, rhythm and pace are incredibly important in my work. While I don't necessarily claim to write poetically, there are times when a I need a word with a certain amount of syllables to make the sentence flow. ChatGPT can easily account for that. Take the chat in Fig 1.2, where I asked for only three-syllable synonyms for 'unhappy.' This feature is vital to me and helps ensure that my writing maintains its unique voice.

Fig 1.2

Good morning. Please could you tell me any three syllable words or group of words, that have the same meaning as unhappy?

Good morning! Here are some three-syllable words or phrases that have a similar meaning to "unhappy":

1. Miserable
2. Discontented
3. Dissatisfied
4. Unfulfilled
5. Melancholic
6. Disheartened
7. Dejected
8. Unfortunate
9. Woebegone
10. Wretched

This makes me happy. To know that I have the word I want at the rhythm I feel my writing requires. (Although, as you will see throughout the book ChatGPT does make mistakes; some of these words actually have four syllables.) But wait, there's more still! (I have the feeling I'm going to repeat that phrase a lot in this book. I should probably put it into ChatGPT to find some alternatives!)

You know when there's a word on the tip of your tongue, but you can't quite remember what it is or if it's the exact word you want? A traditional thesaurus can't help with that, but ChatGPT can. You can tell it the meaning of a word and it will give you the word. Essentially using it as a reverse dictionary. Have a look at this.

Fig 1.3

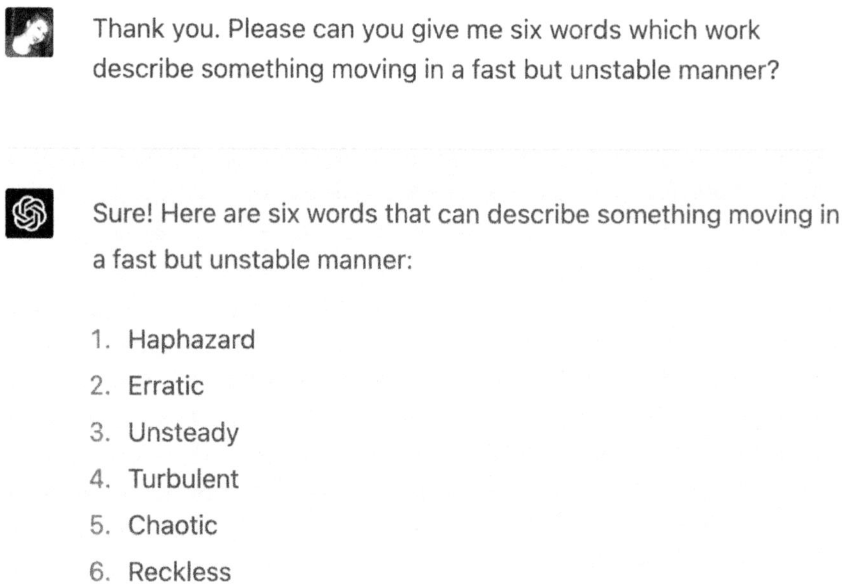

Now, let's go back to the word on the tip of your tongue. It can be highly irritating, especially when writing a first draft. You don't want to stop and get out of the flow by leaving your novel and looking up possibilities and several writers I know have the same approach to this. They will leave a marker for that words that they can't quite recall, keeping writing, and return to them at a later date. Some people use square brackets. Others use letter combinations that do not normally appear together in words, like KC or XYZ. I use an asterisk. Now what about when I come to the second draft, and my brain still can figure out what words I want to use?

Well here comes the AI to help us out. Take a look at here.

Fig 1.4

Good morning. I have written a couple of sentences here, but am unable to think of what words fit in correctly in a couple of places. I have marked these missing words with asterisks. Would you please be able to offer some suggestions? The weather was horrendous. Torrents of rain cascaded down the hillside, ** in streams that ** into the roads. With the water that deep, no car was going to make its way across.

Sure, here are some possible options for the missing words:

The weather was horrendous. Torrents of rain cascaded down the hillside, **turning** in streams that **merged** into the roads. With the water that deep, no car was going to make its way across.

OR

The weather was horrendous. Torrents of rain cascaded down the hillside, **forming** in streams that **pooled** into the roads. With the water that deep, no car was going to make its way across.

OR

The weather was horrendous. Torrents of rain cascaded down the hillside, **flowing** in streams that **converged** into the roads. With the water that deep, no car was going to make its way across.

It doesn't give me one, but three suggestions, straight off, meaning I can pick and choose, or possibly my brain will recall the word it was thinking of it the first place. Either way it's a brilliant tool to have.

2. USING AI TO AID YOUR RESEARCH

Having heard about using AI writing technology at a self-publishing conference in London in 2022 I went back, and immediately had a play on SudoWrite, which was the program the presenter showed us at the time. For the next couple of days, I played around, enjoying the interesting features, and basically seeing it as a little bit of fun. Never did I think that I would actually use AI productively in my writing. If anything, I felt it was a bit of a time-suck, kind of like one of those addictive games on the phone. (I'm not allowed games on my phone anymore. I get way too obsessed and waste too much precious writing time.) However, in November the same year, my husband went to another conference, this time in Vegas. That was when he came back talking about ChatGPT.

Having had my brief dalliance with AI, I decided that I really wasn't that interested. I didn't want to lose any more of my precious writing hours playing with something that I believed would have no long-term benefit. Well, it turned out I was wrong.

It was initially the application of ChatGPT in assisting with one of my least favourite aspects of indie writing that piqued my interest. Marketing. In particular, creating ad copy. What it produced wasn't perfect, not even close, but I could see the potential. Still, I didn't want to be swallowed up by the time commitment of learning to use it.

That changed when I was having a writing breakfast with a friend of mine. For several years she has been determined to write a novel, but time constantly got away from her. So, to make sure she carved out time, we dedicated our Saturday mornings, while both our children are at a club, to write together. We typically spend a couple of hours in a café beavering away away, me with my green tea and her with her hot chocolate. This day, however, green tea wasn't enough. I had a full (veggie) English breakfast, for one very simple reason. I was hungover. I am not a big drinker. I hate the way I am less productive the next day after a couple of glasses of wine — this situation is a case in point of that — but it didn't change the fact that I had had one too many the night before, and my brain wasn't functioning properly. So, wanting to be productive, but knowing anything I wrote that morning would likely be drivel, I turned my attention to something else. Research.

One thing I probably should've mentioned earlier is that I write in more than one genre. My primary genres are rom-coms and historical fiction. While both require research, I'm sure you can immediately understand that one requires a lot more than the other. In fact, the research part of my historical fiction novels probably takes half the time of writing them. So, there I was, working on my new book, needing the layout and structure of a typical house of the time. If I was at home on my desktop, I would have many screenshots of buildings, houses, palaces and places of worship from all the areas I would be writing about. I find homes in particular a nightmare to describe because I am so worried about getting things wrong.

I opened up a webpage on a popular search engine, only to hesitate. I'd been talking to my friend that morning about how much fun ChatGPT was, laughing away at its terrible plot fails. However, I thought I would try and use it to research one of the aspects of my novel. Living areas in homes of the Victorian era. The moment the page began to fill my jaw dropped. What ChatGPT gave me in minutes, would have taken me hours of trawling through webpages and piecing together to get exactly what I wanted, but I didn't stop there. This wasn't enough information for me, so based on the above, I started to ask it more questions, identifying features, building materials, fabrics. Anything I could think of. I was hooked. Something I had dismissed as nothing more than a fad was a real tool that I could use to help me not just write books, but write better researched books. And don't be mistaken into thinking it's only of use to historical fiction writers.

One of my rom-com series is based on a boat, and I needed to know whether or not I would be able to fix a broken propeller without taking the boat out of the water.

Now, I tend to have options: I have friends who live or have once lived on a boat, that I can ask, I can head down to my local marina where the volunteers there are very happy to help me (and I am always exceptionally grateful for their time), or I can telephone random boat yards and marinas to ask the kind ladies and gentlemen there. Thankfully, people who work in the boating industry seem to be very kind and patient, and I haven't had anyone hang up on me yet. I also have the internet of course, but as we all know, this can be incredibly time consuming wading through website after website, then checking the information is up to date.

ChatGPT sorts through all of this for you gives you exactly what you need.

Here's an example: researching how chocolate is made (it's not for actual research, I just love chocolate!).

Fig 2.1

Good afternoon. Please can you describe the process of making chocolate?

Good afternoon! I'd be happy to describe the process of making chocolate. The production of chocolate can be divided into several main stages: harvesting and fermentation, drying, roasting, grinding and conching, tempering, and molding. Each stage plays a crucial role in developing the characteristic flavor and texture of the final product.

1. Harvesting and Fermentation:
   Chocolate production begins with the cacao tree (Theobroma cacao). Cacao pods, which contain cacao beans, are harvested from the tree. The pods are cut open, and the beans along with the surrounding pulp are scooped out. The beans are then placed in large containers or spread out on mats to ferment. Fermentation typically lasts 2-7 days, during which the beans undergo chemical changes that help develop the chocolate flavor.

2. Drying:
   After fermentation, the cacao beans need to be dried to reduce their moisture content. They are spread out in the sun or under sheltered areas and turned regularly to ensure even drying. This process can take anywhere from 5-14 days, depending on the weather and drying method.

Side note: You may have noticed how I try to be polite when talking to ChatGPT. There are two reasons for this; one, manners matter, that's why I make my daughter say please and thank you to Alexa, and two, if AI one day takes over the world and subjugates humanity, I want it to remember I was polite to it so It doesn't vaporise me!

Now the summary in Fig 2.1 is the beginning a solid description of a seven points chocolate making process. But what if I want more? Well, then, I simply ask the AI to **pretend to be an expert.** In this case, I wanted a scientific expert. Look how much more detail I get in the explanation in Fig 2.2. I'd wager this is more than the average novelist will need.

Fig 2.2

Thank you. Could you do the descriptions again, but this time, as an expert, including scientific detail?

Of course! As an expert, I'll delve into the scientific aspects of each stage in the chocolate-making process.

1. Harvesting and Fermentation:
   Cacao trees (Theobroma cacao) produce fruit called cacao pods, which contain 20-60 cacao beans surrounded by a sweet, mucilaginous pulp. When the pods are ripe, they're harvested, and the beans and pulp are scooped out. Fermentation occurs spontaneously, initiated by the wild yeasts and bacteria present in the environment. During fermentation, the pulp's sugars are converted into ethanol and lactic acid. These compounds diffuse into the beans, where they trigger chemical reactions that generate precursors for chocolate flavor development. The temperature during fermentation can reach up to 122°F (50°C), which kills the germ within the bean and helps break down proteins and carbohydrates.

So, you can see by asking the AI to be an expert, you get more detail, but it's still not as much as I might want, so at this point, I'm going to narrow my question down.

Fig 2.3

Thank you, this is greatly appreciated, I would just like to know a little more about the harvesting process. How do you know when a pod is ready to be harvested, and how would a person go about doing this?

You're welcome! Knowing when a cacao pod is ready to be harvested and the proper method of harvesting are crucial to obtaining high-quality beans for chocolate production.

1. Determining pod maturity:
   Cacao pods take about 5-6 months to mature after the tree's flowers are pollinated. When pods are ripe, they typically change color and may develop a slightly rough texture. The specific color change depends on the cacao tree variety. For example, pods from the Criollo variety turn from green to yellow or orange, while pods from the Forastero variety may shift from green to deep red or purple. Another way to determine ripeness is by tapping on the pod with a finger or a stick. A ripe pod will produce a dull, somewhat hollow sound, indicating that the beans inside have reached full maturity.
2. Harvesting method:
   Cacao pods grow directly on the trunk and branches of the cacao tree, at varying heights. Harvesting the pods should be done carefully to avoid damaging the tree, which could reduce future yields. Skilled workers typically use a long-handled cutting tool called a "machete" or a "cacao knife" to reach and remove the pods from the tree. The tool's blade is curved and sharp to allow for precise cuts without harming the tree's bark or flower cushions (where new pods will grow).

I'll be honest, I don't know when I would ever need such an in-depth knowledge of chocolate making, but we have now progressed from a few lines description to something than you could probably use to be the next Willy Wonka. This could prove useful when setting scenes, or for our characters' actions, such as tapping the beans before harvesting.

ChatGPT's name provides a clear indication of its purpose, which is to chat. Because of its technical algorithm, it interacts with users in a conversational manner. As you go back and forth it will improve its responses. So don't hesitate to rephrase your questions and spend a little time following up – just as you would when talking to a human.

Let's try some more research, but this time we will approach it from a different angle. Let's look at Science Fiction.

Fig 2.4

Good afternoon, I am writing a science fiction novel about space travel. Can you please tell me what sort of engines would be most suitable for this, and how the each work?

Good afternoon! I'd be happy to help. There are several types of propulsion systems that you could use in your science fiction novel for space travel. Here are four popular options, along with brief explanations of how they work:

1. Chemical Rockets:
   The most common type of engine used for space travel today is the chemical rocket. It relies on the combustion of chemical propellants (typically a fuel and an oxidizer) to produce a high-pressure gas, which is then expelled through a nozzle to generate thrust. Chemical rockets provide high thrust but are relatively inefficient, as they carry both fuel and oxidizer and have a limited specific impulse (a measure of fuel efficiency).
2. Ion Thrusters:
   Ion thrusters use electric fields to accelerate ions (charged particles) to create thrust. They have a much higher specific impulse than chemical rockets, making them more fuel-efficient. However, ion thrusters produce relatively low thrust, so they are better suited for long-duration missions with low acceleration requirements. There are several types of ion thrusters, such as the Hall-effect thruster and the gridded electrostatic ion thruster.

I've only shown two of the four it suggested, but straight away, I appreciated that all the engines mentioned are based on current or theoretical scientific principles. There are no completely random engines, such as a quark-hydroxide thruster or other similar ideas that are sometimes seen in sci-fi. This attention to scientific realism is essential for readers to be fully immersed in the world created, as it makes the technologies believable to some extent. With ChatGPT at my disposal, I can take my research to the next level and explore this fascinating topic in greater detail. Let's dive deeper into the possibilities.

Fig 2.5

Thank you. I really like the ion thrusters. Please can you give me a more expert description of how these work, and also a comprehensive list of any issues that you could see in using them in a science fiction environment?

Certainly! Ion thrusters are a form of electric propulsion that generate thrust by accelerating ions (charged particles) using electric fields. Here's a more detailed explanation of how they work:

An ion thruster typically consists of three main components: an ionization chamber, an accelerator system, and a neutralizer.

1. Ionization chamber: Inside the ionization chamber, a gas (usually a noble gas like xenon) is introduced and ionized. The ionization process can be achieved through various means, such as electron bombardment, radio-frequency (RF) fields, or microwave energy. The result is a plasma containing positively charged ions and free electrons.

2. Accelerator system: The accelerator system consists of a series of electrodes, which are charged to create electric fields. These fields accelerate the ions, expelling them at high velocities from the thruster. The most common types of ion thrusters are gridded electrostatic ion thrusters and Hall-effect thrusters. In gridded thrusters, ions are accelerated through a set of grids with applied voltages. In Hall-effect thrusters, a magnetic field is used to trap electrons, creating an electric field that accelerates ions.
3. Neutralizer: As the thruster expels positively charged ions, a neutralizer is used to emit electrons into the exhaust plume. This ensures that the spacecraft remains electrically neutral, preventing an electrical charge build-up that could disrupt the acceleration process or damage the spacecraft.

Now, let's discuss some potential issues and challenges with ion thrusters in a science fiction environment:

1. Low thrust: Ion thrusters generate relatively low thrust compared to chemical rockets, which means slower acceleration. This can be a limiting factor in some scenarios, such as escaping a planet's gravity or engaging in rapid maneuvers.
2. Power requirements: Ion thrusters require a substantial amount of electrical power to operate. This power can be provided by solar panels or nuclear reactors, but these options may have limitations in terms of size, mass, or distance from the sun.

3. Erosion and wear: The accelerating grids in gridded ion thrusters can suffer from erosion due to the high-energy ions passing through them, which may reduce the thruster's lifespan. Hall-effect thrusters may also experience erosion in the discharge channel.
4. Thruster scaling: Ion thrusters typically have a low thrust-to-weight ratio, which can limit their ability to scale up for larger spacecraft or higher thrust applications.
5. Fuel supply: While ion thrusters are highly fuel-efficient, they still require propellant, which must be stored onboard the spacecraft. This can be a constraint in terms of mass and volume, especially for long-duration missions.

Despite these challenges, ion thrusters can be an excellent choice for your science fiction story, especially for long-duration missions, deep-space exploration, or situations where fuel efficiency is crucial.

I must admit, my eyes bulged upon reading some of this, despite not being a science fiction writer. (At the moment.) I was immediately drawn to the second part of the response: the things that could go wrong.

A quick scan of this was all it took to inspire at least four chapters of a potential sci-fi book in my mind: a ship is damaged during a meteoroid storm and forced into an emergency landing on planet with limited sunlight, creating a problem for re-launching. I am confident that there is much more potential for further development in this area, and it is not just limited to research, but also offers the opportunity to explore and inspire various plot ideas. (An area we will be heading next.)

But before we move on to that you need to be very aware that ChatGPT is not infallible. You might remember earlier that I mentioned **ChatGPT gets things wrong.**

This following thread from a discussion with ChatGPT is a pretty long one, but hopefully you'll see why I included it in here.

Fig 2.6

Good morning, can you give me a list of 15 herbs, used in medieval times in the U.K. for medicinal reasons, and their purposes. Thank you.

Good morning! I'd be happy to provide you with a list of 15 herbs commonly used in medieval times in the UK for medicinal purposes, along with their purposes:

1. Chamomile - used to ease stomach ailments, anxiety, and insomnia

2. Sage - used to treat sore throats and digestive issues, as well as to improve memory and cognitive function
3. Lavender - used to treat anxiety, insomnia, and headaches, as well as to soothe skin irritations
4. Comfrey - used to heal wounds and reduce inflammation, as well as to ease joint pain and respiratory issues
5. Yarrow - used to stop bleeding and promote wound healing, as well as to reduce fever and ease menstrual cramps

6. St. John's Wort - used to treat depression and anxiety, as well as to ease nerve pain and inflammation
7. Thyme - used to treat respiratory infections and digestive issues, as well as to boost the immune system
8. Rosemary - used to improve memory and cognitive function, as well as to ease muscle pain and promote hair growth
9. Dandelion - used to detoxify the liver and kidneys, as well as to ease digestive issues and reduce inflammation
10. Echinacea - used to boost the immune system and fight infections, as well as to ease respiratory issues and reduce inflammation
11. Feverfew - used to ease migraines and other types of headaches, as well as to reduce inflammation and fever
12. Garlic - used to boost the immune system and fight infections, as well as to lower blood pressure and cholesterol levels

13. Meadowsweet - used to ease digestive issues, reduce fever, and relieve pain
14. Nettle - used to treat allergies and hay fever, as well as to ease joint pain and urinary issues
15. Valerian - used to treat anxiety, insomnia, and nervousness, as well as to ease menstrual cramps and muscle pain

Please note that this information is for educational purposes only and is not intended to replace medical advice from a qualified healthcare professional.

Did all these grow in the U.K. during medieval times?

Yes, all of the herbs I listed were known to grow in the UK during medieval times. In fact, many of them were native to the region, while others were introduced and naturalized. Medieval herbalists and healers would have been familiar with these plants and their medicinal properties, and would have gathered and prepared them for use in various remedies and treatments. It's worth noting that some of these herbs may have been more commonly used in certain regions or by certain cultures within the UK, and that there were likely other herbs that were used for medicinal purposes as well.

Can you explain to me what yarrow is?

Yes, Yarrow (Achillea millefolium) is a perennial herb that is native to Europe and Asia, but has been naturalized throughout North America and other parts of the world. It is a member of the Asteraceae family and is also known by other common names such as common yarrow, nosebleed plant, and thousand-leaf.

Yarrow has a long history of use as a medicinal herb, dating back to ancient times. Its leaves, flowers, and stems contain a variety of compounds that are believed to have medicinal properties, including anti-inflammatory, antimicrobial, and astringent effects.

Yarrow has been traditionally used to treat a variety of conditions, including wounds, fever, digestive issues, menstrual cramps, and respiratory problems. It is also known for its ability to stop bleeding, and was even used by soldiers on the battlefield to staunch bleeding wounds.

Yarrow is a hardy plant that can thrive in a variety of soil types and climates, and is often used in landscaping as a decorative border plant or groundcover. It can also be used in culinary applications, with its young leaves and flowers being used as a bitter salad green or as a seasoning for meats.

Overall, yarrow is a versatile and useful herb that has been valued for its medicinal properties for centuries.

Thank you. Now Echinacea and Valerian?

Certainly! Echinacea and valerian are two other herbs that were commonly used for medicinal purposes in medieval times.

Echinacea is a flowering plant that is native to North America, and was used by Native American tribes for centuries before being adopted by European settlers. It is also known as purple coneflower, and its root, leaves, and flowers are all used for medicinal purposes.

Echinacea is believed to have immune-boosting properties, and is commonly used to prevent and treat colds, flu, and other infections. It is also used to reduce inflammation, relieve pain, and improve overall health and well-being. Echinacea is available in a variety of forms, including capsules, tinctures, and teas.

Valerian is a perennial herb that is native to Europe and Asia, and has been used for medicinal purposes since ancient times. Its root is the part of the plant that is used medicinally, and it is believed to have sedative and anxiolytic effects.

Valerian is commonly used to treat anxiety, insomnia, and nervousness, and is also used as a natural remedy for menstrual cramps and other types of pain. It is available in a variety of forms, including capsules, tinctures, and teas.

It's worth noting that while these herbs were commonly used in medieval times, their effectiveness and safety have not been extensively studied by modern medical research. As with any herbal remedy, it's important to talk to a healthcare professional before using echinacea, valerian, or any other herb for medicinal purposes, especially if you have a pre-existing medical condition or are taking other medications.

So would Echinacea been in the U.K. during medieval times?

No, Echinacea is not native to the UK and would not have been present in the region during medieval times. Echinacea is a flowering plant native to North America and was not introduced to Europe until the 17th century, after the medieval period.

However, it is worth noting that there were likely other herbs used for similar purposes in the UK during medieval times. Medieval herbalists would have relied on native plants and those that were introduced to the region for medicinal purposes. Some of these plants have been lost over time, while others are still used today in traditional herbal medicine.

So the first list you offered was not entirely correct?

I apologize for any confusion. While some of the herbs in the first list, such as chamomile, sage, lavender, and thyme, were commonly used in the UK during medieval times, it is true that Echinacea is not native to the region and would not have been present during that time period.

As an AI language model, my responses are generated based on patterns found in the text data used to train me, and occasionally errors or inaccuracies may occur. I strive to provide the most accurate and helpful information possible, and I appreciate your feedback and questions that allow me to clarify and improve my responses.

If you didn't feel like reading through that whole exchange, what I'm showing you here is that ChatGPT got something wrong. I switched from Sci-fi to talk about something non-fictional. I asked for herbs, solely available in the medieval U.K. Even when it gave the list, I checked with it, wanting confirmation that this selection all were native to the U.K. and it assured me the list was correct. It was only when I doubled down – trying the specific herbs, that I didn't think were right (I was wrong with the yarrow, but I got their eventually) did it finally admit that it had made a mistake. Echinacea would not have been in the U.K. at this time. Who knows, if I went through the entire list, I could well find others that do not fit what I am asking for.

This is not a one-off example. Don't take that to mean that ChatGPT constantly throws up a list of falsehoods, but it is not that unusual either.

Just like those annoying typos that survive seven rounds of proof-edits (I personally celebrate these resilient little buggers now), there will be occasional inaccuracies in research, even for those of us that are as thorough as we can be. But what I hope you see from this, is that assuming whatever answer given to you by any AI after one question is an acceptable level of research for a book you want people to pay their hard-earned money for, is, in my opinion, not an ethical writer's approach. Which is what we are aiming for here. So use it. Absolutely use it. But check it too. If it feels off, check it. If it is vital to your story that the information is correct, check it. If it seems unlikely, check it. Our readers do not deserve work that has not been correctly fact-checked.

3. PLOTTING YOUR BOOK

THIS IS PROBABLY GOING TO BE THE MOST CONTROVERSIAL CHAPTER and if you make the decision to use ChatGPT to help you plot, you need to remember something vital.

The AI is working on data and information that is already out there.

So, here's the issue that everyone worries about. If it is using data that is already there, does that mean you are going to end up with someone else's novel. I'll let you decide on that after you've read this chapter, but first I want you to answer a couple of questions. How many romcoms have a case of mistaken identity? How many thrillers have someone on the inside, a trusted friend even, who turns out not to be that trustworthy? How many space operas have a bounty hunter? Plenty, because what I have described there are tropes. Your job as a writer is to use the tropes, to create something new and original, and that needs to be stressed, because if you can't do that, then your use of AI won't help you.

Now I love plotting. It is, at times, as addictive as writing full novels. (I'm sure many of you have dozens of unfinished first drafts under your belts who can testify to this.) With nearly twenty full-length novels published and several more on their way or discarded before publishing, I have become substantially faster at plotting than I was. I progressed from years, to months, to weeks to get a solid plot down. However, I also have a secret weapon: my spouse.

Please understand, my partner is not a writer and does not always come up with brilliant plot ideas, but he does always offer suggestions for my latest plots (whether I ask for them or not!) and is always available to bounce ideas off. Even when his suggestions are not quite right, they still help me see the direction I want my story to go. While I am fortunate to have this resource, I understand that not everyone has the same privilege. Some writers may feel embarrassed to ask for help with plotting ideas, while others may simply not have anyone who can offer reasonable suggestions. This is where ChatGPT comes in handy, particularly when you find yourself struggling with what I call "plot block." For example, if you were writing a science-fiction novel where the protagonist is trapped on an enemy cargo ship and needs to escape to rescue a kidnapped nephew from an alien king, you could turn to ChatGPT for inspiration.

Fig 3.1

Good morning. I am writing a science fiction novel, and the protagonist is trapped in the cargo hold of an enemy spaceship, with no weapons. Please give ten suggestions for how he might escape.

Good morning! Here are ten suggestions for how your protagonist might escape from the cargo hold of an enemy spaceship:

1. Use the ship's computer system: If the protagonist is tech-savvy, they might be able to hack into the ship's computer system and find a way to unlock the cargo hold doors or even take control of the ship remotely.
2. Use their surroundings: The cargo hold is likely to contain various objects that could be used as weapons or tools. The protagonist could try to fashion a weapon or tool out of these objects and use it to escape.
3. Create a distraction: The protagonist could try to create a distraction that would draw the attention of the crew away from the cargo hold. This could be anything from setting off an alarm to starting a fire.
4. Look for weaknesses in the ship: If the protagonist is knowledgeable about spaceship mechanics, they might be able to identify a weakness in the ship that could be exploited to escape.
5. Signal for help: If the protagonist has access to any kind of communication device, they could try to send a distress signal to allies who could come to their aid.

6. Wait for an opportunity: The protagonist could bide their time and wait for an opportunity to present itself, such as the crew leaving the ship unattended.
7. Stage a mutiny: If there are other prisoners in the cargo hold, the protagonist could try to convince them to stage a mutiny and take control of the ship.

8. Use their own skills: The protagonist might have skills or abilities that could help them escape. For example, if they are an expert in hand-to-hand combat, they could try to overpower the guards.
9. Find a secret passage: The cargo hold might contain a secret passage that the protagonist could use to escape undetected.
10. Create a diversion: The protagonist could create a diversion that would draw the guards away from the cargo hold, such as setting off an explosion in another part of the ship.

Let's be honest, none of these suggestions immediately made me jump out of my seat and say, 'Hooray, this is how I solve the problem!' or think that this is the most genius idea every created. Is there anything there that I couldn't have come up with myself with a little bit of effort? No. However, these points do offer me ideas to start thinking about. Some of the suggestions are immediately ridiculous and will be dismissed, while others are a little bit ridiculous but could be tweaked into something workable. Has AI taken my job of writing for me? Absolutely not. But have I used this technology to avoid wasting an hour of my time staring at a blank screen or typing something I know I'm going to delete later? Yes, hopefully I have. This is just one example of dealing with plot block.

But what about plotting an entire book? Can I use AI for that? Well, the answer is both yes and no from both a practical and ethical view point. Let's switch genres to a popular one at the moment, cosy mystery. I'm going to ask the computer to generate plot points for a cosy mystery novel, and we'll see what it comes up with. Hopefully, this will shed some light on the potential uses and limitations of AI in writing. And why, as I keep trying to stress, AI is here to be a tool for your writing, not do it for you. There are a couple of ways I think are great to help you.

Fig 3.2

Good afternoon. Please can you give me the key points for plotting a cosy mystery novel?

Certainly! Here are some key points to consider when plotting a cozy mystery novel:

1. Set the scene: Introduce your setting and your main character(s). Make sure the reader can envision the setting and get a sense of your main character's personality and backstory.
2. Establish the mystery: A cozy mystery typically involves a crime, often a murder, that needs to be solved. Introduce the mystery early on and provide enough clues to keep the reader engaged, but not enough to give away the solution.
3. Create suspects: Develop a cast of characters who could have committed the crime, including some who may have motives for doing so. Be sure to provide red herrings to keep the reader guessing.
4. Develop the investigation: Your main character(s) should begin investigating the crime, interviewing suspects and gathering clues. Consider adding some twists and turns to keep the reader engaged.
5. Include humor: Cozy mysteries often have a lighthearted tone and include humor. Incorporate witty banter, funny situations, and quirky characters to lighten the mood.
6. Reveal the solution: At the end of the novel, reveal the identity of the culprit and explain how they committed the crime. Make sure the solution is logical and satisfying to the reader.

7. Wrap up loose ends: Tie up any loose ends and provide a resolution for your main character(s). Consider leaving a hint or teaser for the next book in the series.

Remember, these are just some key points to consider when plotting a cozy mystery novel. The specifics will depend on your story and characters, but hopefully this gives you a good starting point. Good luck with your writing!

So once again there is nothing earth shattering here. It's giving me the key points of a cosy mystery novel, which to be fair I could find with a basic Internet search. So, what's an advantage of using the AI over this? Or getting a book on how to plot cosies? (There are plenty of those for sale.)

Even if I am slightly more specific, adding a protagonist and a setting it really doesn't give me that much more.

Fig 3.3

Thank you. Please can you plot a cosy mystery set in a Cornish village, where the main character is a sixty year old dog walker and her best friend lives as a reclusive life, crocheting?

Sure! Here's a possible plot outline for a cozy mystery set in a Cornish village with a 60-year-old dog walker as the main character and her reclusive best friend who enjoys crocheting:

1. Set the scene: Introduce the quaint Cornish village where the story takes place. The main character, Maggie, is a 60-year-old dog walker who loves her job and knows everyone in the village. She has a best friend named Ruth who lives in a small cottage on the outskirts of town and spends most of her time crocheting.
2. Establish the mystery: One of the village's residents, a wealthy retired businessman, is found dead in his mansion. The police rule it as a suicide, but Maggie has her doubts. She starts to investigate the death, looking for clues and interviewing suspects.
3. Create suspects: Maggie discovers that the businessman had several enemies, including his ex-wife who stood to gain a large inheritance from his death, a disgruntled former employee who was fired from the businessman's company, and a rival business owner who was trying to put him out of business.
4. Develop the investigation: Maggie enlists the help of her reclusive friend Ruth, who has a talent for noticing details that others miss. Together, they start to piece together the clues and uncover a hidden motive for the murder.

5. Include humor: Maggie and Ruth have a quirky and humorous friendship, and their interactions throughout the investigation add some light-hearted moments to the story.
6. Reveal the solution: Maggie and Ruth eventually uncover the true culprit, who turns out to be the businessman's ex-wife, who had faked her own death and had been living in the mansion under a false identity.

7. Wrap up loose ends: Maggie and Ruth are able to bring the killer to justice, and the village is able to move on from the tragedy. Maggie continues to walk dogs, and Ruth goes back to her crocheting, content in the knowledge that they were able to solve the mystery.

This is just one possible plot outline, and of course, there are many ways to customize the story to fit your writing style and characters. Happy writing!

I, as the writer, am still going to have to decide what those inside jokes are, or what the details the others miss will be.

So, here's a different approach. Rather than asking the AI to give me a book plot, I'm asking for chapter headings for 30 chapters. As writers, we know what the sweet spot in our plot plans is. (If you are a new writer, this is why I keep saying you have still got to put those hours in.) For me, it's 30 points, and I know that some of those will be split up, so I would normally end up with about 42 chapters. If you're writing a shorter story, pick a value that works better for you. As you can see, I asked ChatGPT for that command, and below is what it came up with.

Fig 3.4

Thank you again. Please can you now give me 30 chapter headings for this book?

Sure, here are 30 possible chapter headings for this cozy mystery novel set in a Cornish village:

1. The Dead Man in the Mansion
2. Maggie Takes on the Case
3. Interviewing the Suspects
4. Ruth's Expertise in Crochet
5. A Clue at the Tea Shop
6. A Mysterious Note
7. A Breakthrough in the Investigation
8. Maggie's Run-In with the Police
9. A Secret Meeting with a Suspect
10. A Threatening Phone Call
11. An Alibi Disproved
12. Ruth's Observations in the Village
13. A Break-In at the Mansion
14. A Conversation with the Ex-Wife

15. The Discovery of a Hidden Room
16. A Suspicious Meeting at the Pub
17. Maggie and Ruth Follow a Lead
18. A Clue in the Crochet Pattern
19. An Unexpected Visit from the Police
20. A New Suspect Emerges
21. A Key Piece of Evidence Found
22. A Risky Plan to Gather Information
23. A Shocking Revelation
24. Maggie and Ruth Put the Pieces Together
25. A Confrontation with the Killer

26. The Killer's Motive is Revealed
27. A Dangerous Situation
28. The Police Arrive to Make an Arrest
29. Wrapping Up Loose Ends
30. Maggie and Ruth's Friendship Stronger Than Ever

Again, these are just one possibility, and you can adjust or modify them to fit your story and characters. Good luck with your writing!

Now this is where people tend to feel like the computer is doing all the work for you. At first glance it appears that we have got a plot for our novel without doing any of the legwork but honestly, let's look at this more closely. The chapter headings feel like they fit into the genre and it has a good idea of the beats of the story, and where the key elements should fit into it. Similarly to if you were to use a guide on something like Plottr.

But there are some issues around pace and timing. Do we really believe each of these headings will last for exactly one chapter? Some seem like they would be much longer, for example with the risky plan, they've got to decide on it, and then carry it out. I feel like the fact it would be risky, means something will go wrong, and this is actually more like two, possibly three chapters, whereas the end one, Maggie and Ruth's friendship is stronger than ever, doesn't tell us a thing. Certainly not enough to warrant a chapter heading. And it still hasn't given us the plot. It is definitely helping us to build one, I won't deny that, but do I think you could hand this list to someone random on the street and expect them to write an even moderately entertaining book? Probably not.

Still, I want to stick with this method of plotting right now and see how we can develop these ideas with ChatGPT, rather than going insane trying to plug the thousand plot holes it has unwillingly created for us. It's time to ask it to expand this for us.

Fig 3.5

Please can you take the previous chapter headings, and give each one a detailed summary outlining all the key points of that chapter in approximately 4 sentences.

Sure, here are some detailed summaries for each chapter of this cozy mystery novel:

1. The Dead Man in the Mansion - Maggie, a 60-year-old dog walker in a Cornish village, discovers the wealthy businessman's body in his mansion and starts to doubt the police's conclusion of suicide.
2. Maggie Takes on the Case - Maggie decides to investigate the businessman's death on her own and begins to interview potential suspects, including the businessman's ex-wife, former employees, and others who may have had a motive for his murder.
3. Interviewing the Suspects - Maggie continues her investigation by questioning the suspects, trying to find out more about their potential involvement in the businessman's murder.
4. Ruth's Expertise in Crochet - Maggie's best friend, Ruth, who is a reclusive crochet enthusiast, offers her unique perspective on the investigation and provides helpful insights.
5. A Clue at the Tea Shop - Maggie and Ruth visit a local tea shop and discover a clue that could help them identify the killer.
6. A Mysterious Note - Maggie receives a mysterious note that hints at the identity of the killer and warns her to stop investigating.

It did all 30 points (albeit not all with four sentences), but I don't want to fill the entire book with my screenshots. After all, I do have to put some work in here too.

Now, taking a look at Fig 3.5, hopefully you can see why I'm not worried about ChatGPT turning everyone with an internet connection into a world class writer.

Rather than developing what was there, it has simply written it out in a longer form, with no added substance. Besides, if you're a writer of cosy mystery novels, you're likely a reader of cosy mystery novels as well. As such, you already know the genre tropes, such as the amateur sleuth, the small village setting, and the overheard conversation that sets things in motion. There is nothing new here and you are still going to need to put in the work.

Let's take the example of the first chapter, titled "The Dead Man in the Mansion." According to ChatGPT, Maggie discovers the wealthy businessman's body and doubts the police's conclusion of suicide. Already, I have a lot of questions that I, as the writer have to be able to answer before I can start to write this book. Why was Maggie at the house? Did she walk his dogs? Why did the police conclude suicide? What did she see that made her doubt it? All of these would be fundamental in the actual plotting of this book. Did she see a broken glass, or a bloody fingerprint? Or was it that the dog's lead was taken off the hook, as if he was about to start walking it. These initial clues will change the trajectory of the entire story, and it's up to the writer to know what they are.

In every chapter the fundamental core which the writer is responsible for is missing. What was the clue in the Tea Shop? What was Ruth's unique perspective? What was written in the mysterious note, and who did it implicate? This same plot could be taken by a hundred authors and none of them would end up with the same story at the end of it. That's the joy of humanity and what AI cannot bring to the table.

So, if you're up in arms about using AI to plot your novel, then are you also objecting to every book or website that provides guidance on novel writing? Those that describe the tropes and characteristics favoured in the different genre? Plotting with AI can be helpful if you're a new writer or need ideas to bounce off, but if you try to turn the suggestions into a book without no writing skills, then I'm afraid you're not going to have a great read at the end of it.

This is where you have to consider its limitations. As I have already mentioned, I see ChatGPT as a format to bounce ideas off and it's a great one, but you have to have your ideas to feedback and respond to. Otherwise, you're going to find yourself in trouble. This is where the ethics part really comes to play. Say I want to write a Middle-grade books based on Greek gods. It's been done a lot, sure, but it's a hugely popular genre, so hopefully the AI will give us something great, right? I'm afraid not.

Fig 3.6

Please can you write me out a six book summary for a new middle grade novel series about the Greek gods, taking prominent roles in children's society. ie teachers, doctors, etc. For each book, give the title, book summary and twelve key points.

Sure, here's a summary for a new middle grade novel series about the Greek gods:

Book 1: "Olympus Elementary: The Godly Teachers"

Summary: The Greek gods and goddesses take on new roles as teachers at Olympus Elementary, a school for demigods. Follow the adventures of a new student, Alex, as he learns from the best teachers in the universe.

Key points:

1. The school is located on Mount Olympus, but it's invisible to mortals.
2. The teachers include Zeus, Hera, Poseidon, Athena, and more.
3. Each god teaches a different subject, like math, science, and history.
4. Alex is a demigod, meaning he's half human and half god.
5. He struggles with controlling his powers and fitting in at school.
6. The other students include children of Greek gods and mortal parents.
7. There's a rivalry between Alex and another student, who's the child of Zeus.
8. The students go on a field trip to the Underworld to learn about Hades.
9. The school has a cafeteria that serves ambrosia and nectar.
10. There's a mysterious creature lurking on the school grounds.
11. Alex and his friends have to work together to save the school from danger.
12. The book ends with a cliffhanger that sets up the next book in the series.

This is not good. It's basically trying to get me to re-write the Percy Jackson series, which is not what I want. But at the same time it's not surprising. AI will tell you that it is using the patterns and information given to it, to try to develop something new, but if there is not much information for it to turn too, then it's not going to be able to add any variety. Percy Jackson is the biggest middle-grade series about Greek gods out there, so all of the AI's resources and data, are going to tell it that this what we want. If we want something original, we've got to give it something original, and that's where we as creatives come in.

In this next prompt, I ask it to include some specific points, and give it free rein to use its imagination in others, to see how well it could find a threat to fit in with my heroes. Have a look at how different this is when I give it more to work with.

Fig 3.7

Thank you but I think we need something more original than a demi-god at school for gods and children. To start with, I want to the lead to be a female 12 year old, total human. No connections to the gods at all. It needs to be set in London. I only want one god to be a teacher, the others need different jobs — please list them and find suitable jobs for their powers – the female lead must keep the gods a secret, after discovering what these people are, and the threat is not to the school but to something different. She discovered the gods secret, when she was trying to help her mother by earning money. Please give an explanation of what all these things are before you continue with the story and the plot.

Certainly, here's a new summary for a middle grade novel series about the Greek gods:

Book 1: "London's Secret Gods"

Summary: When 12-year-old Emily discovers a secret world of Greek gods living among humans in London, she becomes entangled in a dangerous mystery that could change the fate of the world. With the help of a powerful but eccentric teacher and the gods themselves, Emily must navigate a treacherous path to save the city from a threat beyond imagination.

Key points:

1. Emily is a total human with no connections to the gods.
2. The story is set in London, where the gods have taken on different jobs to blend in with humans.
3. Only one god, Apollo, is a teacher at Emily's school, teaching music.
4. The other gods have different jobs that match their powers, such as:

- Athena works as a detective, using her intelligence and strategy to solve cases.
- Hermes runs a delivery service, able to move quickly and efficiently through the city.
- Demeter runs a community garden, using her powers to help plants grow and feed the city.
- Hephaestus is a blacksmith, creating powerful weapons and gadgets for the gods.
- Dionysus owns a restaurant and bar, creating delicious and potent drinks for his patrons.

5. Emily discovers the gods' secret while working at a market to earn money for her family.
6. She witnesses Apollo using his powers to heal a wounded bird, revealing his true identity.
7. Apollo tells Emily about the other gods and their secret lives in London.
8. Emily is sworn to keep the gods' secret, but she becomes embroiled in a dangerous plot.
9. Someone is using powerful artifacts to try and control the gods and bend them to their will.
10. Emily must work with the gods and Apollo's eccentric brother, Dionysus, to uncover the plot and stop the threat.
11. The story explores themes of friendship, trust, and the power of mythology in modern times.
12. The book ends with a cliffhanger, setting up the next book in the series.

Now, this is better. It did what I asked in terms of the gods having regular jobs which fit in with their powers, some of them in particular, like Dionysus owning a bar. I know If I wanted to add a couple more gods into the mix, it would provide them fairly easily too.

But then let's look at the plot itself. Again, we need to do all the leg work before we could start writing this. "A dangerous plot," "Powerful artefacts." These kind of statements are hugely vague and those last five points, are incredibly generic. As always though, I want to see if we can develop them into anything decent.

Fig 3.8

Thank you. I like your choices of characters but would like to see them more involved in the story. Please can you take all points after point seven, and re-write each of these as a detailed paragraph, including explanations at to how the themes are explored, and what the threats might be.

Sure, here's a revised summary for the first book:

Book 1: "London's Secret Gods"

Summary: When 12-year-old Emily discovers a secret world of Greek gods living among humans in London, she becomes entangled in a dangerous mystery that could change the fate of the world. With the help of a powerful but eccentric teacher and the gods themselves, Emily must navigate a treacherous path to save the city from a threat beyond imagination.

Key points:

1. Emily is a total human with no connections to the gods.

Emily is an ordinary 12-year-old girl living in London. She is a bit of a loner and has trouble making friends at school. She spends most of her time helping her mother, who is struggling to make ends meet. Emily is resourceful, curious, and has a strong sense of justice.

2. The story is set in London, where the gods have taken on different jobs to blend in with humans.

The gods have taken on different roles in modern-day London to blend in with humans. They have jobs that match their powers and personalities, such as Athena working as a detective, Hermes running a delivery service, and Demeter running a community garden. Emily is fascinated by the idea of gods living among humans and tries to learn more about them.

It has definitely given us more of an insight into our protagonist, but despite the fact I asked for more detail it hasn't actually added that much more depth to the plot. It's just expanded the number of words that it's included. The same as it did with the cosy mystery. And the same happens again when I ask for it to expand the first chapters.

Fig 3.9

Thank you. Can you add more detail to the first three chapters. Give 12 key points for each of them.

Sure, here are more detailed descriptions of the first three chapters of "London's Secret Gods":

Chapter 1: "Emily's Discovery"

Key points:

1. Emily is introduced as an ordinary 12-year-old girl living in London who has trouble making friends at school.
2. She spends most of her time helping her mother, who is struggling to make ends meet.
3. Emily is curious and has a strong sense of justice.
4. She is working at a market to earn money when she witnesses Apollo using his powers to heal a wounded bird.
5. Emily is shocked to discover that Apollo is a god.
6. She becomes determined to learn more about him and the other gods.
7. Emily starts to investigate Apollo's background.
8. She discovers that he is a music teacher at her school.
9. Emily becomes fascinated by the idea of gods living among humans.
10. She tries to learn more about the other gods and their powers.
11. Emily struggles with the decision of whether to keep the gods' secret or reveal it to the world.
12. The chapter ends with Emily feeling conflicted and unsure about what to do next.

I have reached a point here where it keeps expanding the same points, without any additional depth and what it does add, doesn't always make sense in its given context. Somehow this jam-packed chapter is missing a few key elements, like how Emily comes to the conclusion that Apollo is a god, not a healer, or a wizard. And I can't help but think she would know he was a music teacher at her school too.

Basically, when it comes to plotting, the better quality of ideas we give it, the better responses it will help us with. In fact, ChatGPT will happily tell you that in order to get it to do a good plot, you need to give it a lot. If you have a look at Fig 3.10, you will see that rather than beating around the bush and getting wishy-washy plots I went straight to the horse's mouth and asked ChatGPT what it required to produce a fantastic plot. And the response shouldn't be a surprise.

Fig 3.10

I want you to write a plot for a fantastic story for me. What information should I give you in order to ensure that the plot is as detailed and interesting as possible?

In order to create a detailed and interesting plot for your story, I would need to know the following information:

1. Genre: What genre are you interested in writing? Is it science fiction, fantasy, romance, mystery, thriller, or a combination of genres?
2. Setting: Where does the story take place? Is it set in a futuristic world, a magical kingdom, a small town, or a big city? The setting can greatly affect the plot and the mood of the story.
3. Characters: Who are the main characters in your story? What are their personalities, backgrounds, and motivations? Knowing your characters in depth can help shape the plot and create compelling conflicts.

4. Conflict: What is the main conflict in your story? Is it an internal conflict, such as a character struggling with their own beliefs or emotions, or an external conflict, such as a war or a mystery to solve? The conflict is the driving force of the plot and should be well-defined and engaging.
5. Theme: What is the underlying message or theme of your story? Is it about love, loss, redemption, or something else? The theme can provide depth and meaning to the plot and help tie everything together.
6. Plot Points: Are there any specific plot points or events that you want to include in your story? For example, a plot twist or a dramatic confrontation. These elements can help create tension and excitement in the plot.

With this information, I can create a plot that is tailored to your preferences and captures the essence of your story.

By the time you hit point 3, you can see it's asking you for a lot. In fact, it's saying you need to know everything about your characters and all the obstacles they are going to face. Bluntly put, ChatGPT knows that you need to do a ton of work if you're going to get it to create something good. Bad news for the get-rich-quick brigade who think it will do everything for them, but hopefully reassuring for those of you that think it's going to destroy the craft of writing in the next six months. You as a storyteller are the difference.

But before we finish plotting, I want to show you a couple of tricks where ChatGPT can be useful. These tools I genuinely think can help you, particularly if you are stuck with where your story needs to go. Rather than trying to get ChatGPT to write a book for you, let's do what I keep telling you it does best, and use it as a soundboard for different ideas. There are couple of ways of doing thing.

What if all you know, is you want to write a thriller book? You love reading them, they are hugely popular, but there are so many sorts out there. You just don't know what you want to do. Even well-established writers can struggle to get started, but ChatGPT can help just by giving you a series of ideas to go with.

Now, yes, you can find a list like this in lots of places on the internet which have similar, if less extensive lists, but again, the advantage is you can personalise it.

Fig 3.11

Can you give me 100 different devices that could happen in a thriller novel. Thank you

Certainly! Here are 100 different devices that could happen in a thriller novel:

1. Kidnapping
2. Murder
3. Blackmail
4. Identity theft
5. Cybercrime
6. Espionage
7. Terrorist attack
8. Hostage situation
9. Conspiracy
10. Corruption

It did do as I asked, and gave me a list of a hundred, but that takes up way too much space, so you'll just have to believe me.

A quick scan down the list and you know it is spot on, but a good thriller is going to contain many of these plot devices, linked seamlessly together. Can ChatGPT do that?

Fig 3.12

With the list of thriller devices give above, please can you narrow it to twenty which could happen in the UK, and add a one sentence summary of what could happen.

Sure! Here are twenty thriller devices that could happen in the UK, along with a one-sentence summary of what could happen:

1. Political scandal - A government official is caught in a bribery scandal involving a major corporation, with dire consequences for all involved.
2. Identity theft - A victim's identity is stolen and used to commit a series of increasingly serious crimes, leading them on a desperate hunt for the thief.
3. Assassination plot - A plot to assassinate a high-profile public figure is uncovered, and a race against time ensues to thwart the plan and bring the conspirators to justice.
4. Cyberattack - A cyberattack on a major financial institution or government agency results in widespread chaos and destruction, with devastating consequences for society.

Now in my opinion, this list (which actually contained 20 suggestions) is more useful than anything else that I've shown you in the plotting chapter so far. It has given me a selection of ideas that I can use to *build* a plot. Now, I'm sure that immediately there are going to be those out there, that are asking *Can't I just get it to plot for me.* Well, let's have a look, because what I'm trying to show people who think it can do their job for them, is that's not going to happen.

Fig 3.13

Amazing. Thank you. Can you now take nine of these and weave them together into a plot for a novel, with a old female detective?

Certainly! Here's a potential plot for a novel featuring an old female detective and incorporating nine of the thriller devices listed above:

Detective Inspector Maeve MacIntyre thought she had seen it all in her long career with the police force. But when a series of seemingly unrelated incidents began to pile up, she realized that something sinister was afoot.

It started with a cyberattack on a major financial institution, causing widespread panic and chaos. The bank's security protocols had been breached, and millions of pounds had been siphoned off by unknown criminals. Maeve was called in to investigate, and soon discovered that the attack was just the beginning.

As she delved deeper, she uncovered a web of corruption and conspiracy, implicating high-ranking government officials, corporate executives, and organized crime syndicates. She knew that she was in over her head, but Maeve was never one to back down from a challenge.

The investigation led Maeve to a shadowy figure known only as "The Dealer," who operated a vast drug trafficking network across the country. The Dealer was always one step ahead of Maeve and her team, but she refused to give up.

Meanwhile, a serial killer was on the loose, targeting young women in the city. Maeve knew that time was running out to catch the killer before they struck again.

In the midst of it all, Maeve's personal life was falling apart. She had recently discovered that her daughter had been the victim of identity theft, and the culprit was still at large. Maeve was torn between her duty to the investigation and her desire to protect her family.

The case came to a head when Maeve discovered a plot to assassinate a high-profile public figure, orchestrated by a terrorist organization with links to The Dealer's drug trafficking network. Maeve knew that she had to act quickly to prevent disaster.

> With the help of her team, Maeve uncovered evidence of the plot and thwarted the assassination attempt just in time. The investigation led to a tense standoff with The Dealer, who was finally brought to justice for their crimes.
>
> In the end, Maeve emerged victorious, but at a great personal cost. She had sacrificed everything to bring down The Dealer and protect the people of her city. As she retired from the police force, Maeve knew that she had done her duty, but wondered if it had all been worth it in the end.

So, at first glance, this looks like it's given us a very comprehensive plot outline, but has it really? If we break down, what it usable and how much do we need to add ourselves?

Again, we are facing the same issues that we have seen throughout this chapter; there is no substance to the plot.

Starting with an embezzlement case would be sound enough, but what is making her dig deep in the first place? There has to be something happen to cause her to react in that way. And what is the web that's going to bring down the entire government? A dangerous game of political intrigue? What does that mean? It might sound good on the blurb of a book, but for a plot, we need specifics. We need to know how she discovered the links between The Network and foreign governments. We need to know how they identified killings as being linked to a serial killer and if or how they caught them.

It does add to the character development, with her marriage falling apart, but in all honesty, this reads like a long blurb, meant to entice a reader, rather than an actual plot. To turn it into something useable, you are going to have to do the bulk of the work yourself. And that's okay. That is what we are meant to do as writers. Be the storyteller.

Summarising using ChatGPT on plotting.

It's great for offering ideas to incorporate into your plot, but not so good at fully plotting.

It will use ideas based on well-known successful stories out there, so you need to be aware of that. You will have to bring the originality.

4. CHATGPT AND CHARACTERS

HAVING CHARACTERS YOUR READER CAN INVEST IN IS KEY TO A GOOD book. Characters you can feel empathy for or despise. Good guys, bad guys, we need them both. But before we get on to any complexities in our characters' natures we are going to start simpler than that. Names.

I don't know about you, but I hate making up names. For some reason, I can only think of names beginning with vowels, or vowel sounds and as such I always seem to end up with three characters in the same book all starting their names with the same letter. Fortunately, that's not going to happen to me anymore.

Now of course, you can just ask ChatGPT to create names for you.

Fig 4.1

Good evening. Please can you give me ten name suggestions of a fiction British female police officer, in her mid-forties. Thank you.

ChatGPT

Certainly, here are ten name suggestions for a fictional British female police officer in her mid-forties:

1. Detective Inspector Olivia Smith
2. Detective Chief Inspector Rachel Collins
3. Detective Superintendent Emma Williams
4. Detective Inspector Kate Harris
5. Detective Sergeant Claire Watson
6. Detective Chief Superintendent Sarah Jones
7. Detective Inspector Lucy Davies
8. Detective Superintendent Laura Brown
9. Detective Sergeant Karen Green
10. Detective Chief Inspector Jane Bennett

That's handy, if like me you're rubbish at names, though by putting British in, they seem a bit English-centric. Still, while this is useful what's even better, is when you need names from a country or region you are not familiar with.

Fig 4.2

Good evening. Please can you give me ten name suggestions of a fiction Thai female police officer, in her mid-forties. Thank you

Certainly, here are ten name suggestions for a fictional Thai female police officer in her mid-forties:

1. Lieutenant Colonel Somsri Phromma
2. Captain Sirikanya Thanom
3. Major Somrak Saengdee
4. Inspector Supatra Chaikun
5. Colonel Patcharin Chotisak
6. Lieutenant Nattaya Saengchan
7. Major Nopparat Saetang
8. Captain Pattraporn Suksan
9. Colonel Jiraporn Chalermsuk
10. Lieutenant Chutima Phetcharatana

In generating names like this, in ChatGPT, I no longer run the same risk of using names that are incorrect, or hopefully overused, I can also narrow down the region, so that it is more specific. I can ask it to use names popular in a certain decade or century or even ones that have specific meanings.

Fig 4.3

Good afternoon. Please can you give me 10 suggested names for a character from Edinburgh in the 16th Century.? They are male, twenties, farming and an extremely good-natured person, so please give name meaning that reflect this. Thank you.

Sure, here are 10 suggested names for your character:

1. Angus - means "one strength" in Gaelic
2. Alistair - means "defender of the people" in Scottish Gaelic
3. Finlay - means "fair-haired warrior" in Gaelic
4. Ewan - means "born of the yew tree" in Gaelic
5. Fergus - means "man of force" in Gaelic
6. Lachlan - means "from the land of lakes" in Gaelic
7. Niall - means "champion" in Gaelic
8. Ruairidh - means "red king" in Gaelic
9. Seamus - means "supplanter" in Scottish Gaelic
10. Tavish - means "twin" in Gaelic

I hope these suggestions help you in naming your character!

I'm sure I'm not the only one who will find that incredibly useful.

Now, let's go a little bit deeper than the names and talk about our characters' natures. As a writer, there are certain things you need to keep in mind when developing a character. They need to have flaws – real, human flaws – and conflict in their lives, or at least if you want the book to be remotely interesting. So once again, we can use AI as a sounding board to help us develop those features in our characters. We don't always have to use lists, as I have done up until this point. Sure, lists have a place, but when we need to collect more information, there's seldom a better option than a table.

Fig 4.4

Good afternoon. Please can you create a table of 10 characters for a police thriller set in the highlands. It must have names, ages, occupations, physical description character talents and flaws. Thank you.

Sure, here's a table of 10 characters for a police thriller set in the highlands with their physical descriptions, character talents, and flaws:

Name	Age	Occupation	Physical Description	Character Talents	Flaws
Detective Cameron	42	Detective	Tall and athletic with short dark hair and intense blue eyes	Experienced in criminal investigation, skilled in observation and analysis	Struggles with PTSD from a traumatic experience on the job
Constable Ross	29	Police Officer	Strong and sturdy with a rugged appearance and a thick beard	Physically fit, knowledgeable about the highlands, excellent marksmanship	Can be impulsive and hot-headed, sometimes struggles with authority
Sergeant Robertson	38	Police Sergeant	Fit and muscular with short blonde hair and a no-nonsense demeanor	Experienced in leadership and team management, knowledgeable about law	Can be overly aggressive and prone to violence, struggles with addiction
Forensic Scientist	31	Forensic Scientist	Petite and precise with glasses and a lab coat	Skilled in evidence analysis and DNA testing, knowledgeable about science	Can be socially awkward and detached, struggles with anxiety

Victim's Father	50	Businessman	Well-dressed and dignified with graying hair and piercing blue eyes	Wealthy and influential, knowledgeable about the community	Can be secretive and manipulative, has a strained relationship with his son
Victim's Mother	48	Homemaker	Soft-spoken and caring with a warm smile and a nurturing demeanor	Compassionate and empathetic, knowledgeable about her family	Can be overprotective and meddling, sometimes struggles with anxiety
Witness	25	Waitress	Attractive and bubbly with long curly hair and a bright personality	Observant and detail-oriented, knowledgeable about the local area	Can be easily intimidated and prone to panic, has a history of substance abuse
Suspect	35	Handyman	Scruffy and disheveled with a rugged appearance and rough hands	Skilled in construction and repair work, knowledgeable about the area	Can be volatile and unpredictable, has a history of violent behavior
Attorney	55	Lawyer	Sophisticated and polished with a sharp wit and a commanding presence	Knowledgeable about the law, skilled in negotiation and argumentation	Can be ruthless and unscrupulous, prone to unethical behavior
Journalist	28	Reporter	Sleek and stylish with a confident demeanor and a hunger for the truth	Skilled in investigation and research, knowledgeable about the media	Can be pushy and intrusive, sometimes struggles with ethical boundaries

There is no denying that this is incredible. By asking ChatGPT to put our results in a table, it will do exactly that. It has also filled in the columns with the information that I asked, including those personality traits that are necessary if we are going to develop fully rounded characters.

Without doubt, there are some amazing things on this table, and I'm going to talk about them, but don't worry, critics, I'll be in with the negatives too in a minute.

In a matter of minutes I've got a table that would likely take me far longer to type up myself, but time saving aside, let's talk about other features, positives and negatives.

I have created tables like this on ChatGPT numerous times – often to show other writers how to do it, and this example here that I've chosen is an example where it did not go exactly to plan when it comes to the names. It hasn't actually given me them. Instead, it's given me roles in the book. This was easy to rectify, but I wanted to include it so you could see that not everything works perfectly first time. Even if you have asked for it to do exactly the same thing beforehand. Think of it as a person who is looking at you, and appears to be listening, only for you to discover they were away with the fairies and need you to repeat yourself. (I'm definitely not pointing the finger at my husband here.)

But it's easy enough to cut and paste or re-type the command and with that done, we can have a more detailed look at what it has given us.

Fig 4.5

Good morning. Please can you give me a table of 10 characters for a Thriller set in the Scottish highlands. Include, name, age, occupations, physical appearance, talents and flaws.

Sure, here's a table of 10 characters for a Thriller set in the Scottish highlands:

Name	Age	Occupation	Physical Appearance	Talents	Flaws
Ewan MacKenzie	45	Retired Detective	Tall, rugged, with graying hair and piercing blue eyes	Keen observation skills, expert in profiling and deduction	Struggles with alcoholism and PTSD
Kirsty Campbell	30	Park Ranger	Fit and athletic, with short brown hair and green eyes	Expertise in wilderness survival and tracking	Impulsive and tends to act before thinking
Angus MacPherson	55	Farmer	Stout and muscular, with a thick beard and bushy eyebrows	Skilled in animal husbandry and traditional Scottish music	Prone to anger and has a hot temper

One of my favourite features is the occupations, which I feel go pretty well with the names. I know I have spent hours trying to decide what profession to give certain characters, researching their profession and then changed my mind halfway through a first draft because it didn't quite fit. The same could be said with their personality traits. Now ChatGPT has a list ready for me which I can pick and choose from or move to another character as I see fit. This is very much research and thinking time, sped up. I am impressed by the way skills and talents also match the occupations. Same with the flaws, although some could say that that is predictable. I also like the way some of the flaws are not something I would have immediately considered.

What about the negatives. While you can't see it in this table, unfortunately, three people out of ten people had the same surname. There's no way anything with an ounce of common sense would think to do that unless the characters are related. However, this a further concern, a much bigger one, one which you can't tell simply by looking at the table.

I ran this prompt four times, with my free login, my paid and my husband's and then again over a month later. ***Each time*** Detective Ewan McKenzie came up top. When I ask my friend to do it — again, Saturday writing session — her top character DI Ewan McLeod, who also suffered with alcoholism, had a very similar physical appearance and set of talents and skills. Many of the other characters given were also the same or only slight variations each time, like having a hotel receptionist, rather than Bed and Breakfast owner or a game keep instead of a farmer.

Does this mean if everyone uses ChatGPT we are going to end up with hundreds of books, all with the same characters? Well, here are my thoughts on it. And as I try to get across as much as possible, I am a writer, not a computer expert.

Let's be honest, the reason ChatGPT gave all of us a D.I. with an alcohol problem, is because it's a trope that frequently appears in the genre. Just like the handsome, but surly lead character that has a secret soft side in a rom-com, or the double crossing friend in an adventure story. There will always be familiarity and similarities in genres; after all, it is the tropes that define a genre. That is undeniable. *But* it doesn't change the fact that using the first answer ChatGPT gives you, is lazy and if you do end up with identically names to someone else's book, the pair of you should probably have put more effort into planning.

So, back to the table, we already know there's an issue with the surnames. I will confess to not having that many Scottish friends. I'm from down south, but I probably have a dozen or so that I can rattle off the top of my head. Do you know how many of those have a surname that begins with Mac? One. Maybe my control group isn't reflective of the general population, I'm happy to admit that, but I'm not convinced these are either. And even if they are, having so many similar surnames could be confusing for the reader. This, is again, is where we are going to have to use our knowledge and judgement as writers to realise that not all this information is useable. We know from an earlier chapter how easy it is to get it to give us names, so if you can't think of any for yourself, then go back and generate a list. But there is more than just a name to a character.

Moving on from the names and the table, I want to look more into the personalities of our characters.

Often when we write characters we draw on personality traits that we know best, our own or those of people close to us. It is therefore easy for us to describe how those characters react in familiar situations. But what happens when we need a character to have a personality trait we are unfamiliar with, or who has a wildly different world view to us? What happens when those characters find themselves in places and situations totally alien to us? As a writer, it is our job to place them in unfamiliar situations and ensure they act in a way that is believable. We need to know how each character we have created is going to respond and react in certain situations, and research may well be required.

Fig 4.6

What are character traits of extremely shy people? What situations might they shy away from? What kind of response would crowds give them?

Extremely shy people may exhibit various character traits, although it's important to remember that shyness varies from person to person. Some common traits may include:

1. Social anxiety: Shy individuals often feel anxious or self-conscious in social situations, fearing negative evaluation or judgment.
2. Introversion: They may have a preference for spending time alone or in smaller groups, as they recharge their energy through solitude.
3. Quietness: Shy people tend to speak softly and may not contribute much to conversations.
4. Avoidance: They may avoid eye contact and maintain a distance from others, particularly in unfamiliar environments or with new people.
5. Hesitation: They might take longer to make decisions or respond to questions, as they are more cautious and self-aware.

Extremely shy people might shy away from situations such as:

1. Large social gatherings or parties
2. Public speaking or giving presentations
3. Meeting new people or initiating conversations
4. Asserting their opinions or disagreeing with others
5. Taking the lead in group settings
6. Participating in group discussions or activities
7. Engaging in activities that draw attention to themselves

> Crowds may respond to extremely shy people in various ways, including:
>
> 1. Overlooking them: Due to their quiet and reserved nature, shy individuals may go unnoticed or be excluded from social interactions.
> 2. Misinterpreting their behavior: Some people might misinterpret shyness as aloofness, disinterest, or rudeness.
> 3. Empathy and understanding: Others may recognize their shyness and offer support or encouragement to help them feel more comfortable.
> 4. Curiosity: Some individuals might find the shy person intriguing and want to get to know them better.
> 5. Annoyance or frustration: In some cases, people may become frustrated with the shy person's reluctance to engage in social interactions or contribute to conversations.
>
> It's essential to understand that each shy individual is unique and may experience and exhibit different traits and reactions to situations. To support them, try to be patient, understanding, and empathetic, and give them space and time to open up and feel comfortable.

From that second list there, we immediately have situations that would cause our main characters stress. Besides helping us understand more about our characters' personality, these points could easily be used to help develop our plot, as anything which creates tension is great for moving a plot forward.

I want to finish this chapter with a disclaimer. The information here is based on generalisations and stereotypes. As a rule you don't want your characters to be obvious and lazy stereotypes, you want them to be unique to you. That's where your skill in developing a fully rounded, realistic character comes in. What makes us turn a page or gasp when we are reading are the unpredictable elements. The shy boy being the first to make the move and place the kiss on his crush. The good guy who has pretended to be the bad guy, sacrificing themselves. Humans are nuanced and multi-faceted, don't rely on these rather flat and soulless generations. AI is not capable of creating those nuances for you. You are the person who will have to bring each personality off the page and make sure they balance out to fit the story that you want to tell.

5. CREATING AUTHENTICITY WITH AI

THIS IS NOT GOING TO BE A LONG PART OF THE BOOK, AND MAYBE IT IS not worth its own chapter heading because of how small it is, but it is definitely one of my favourites tools that I have discovered from using AI. Probably because of how bad I am at doing this first part as a writer normally. And here it is. Dialect.

I hate writing dialect. Actually, I avoid it, at almost all costs. A lot of time, when I try to write it, it can come across as cliched, or corny, or just downright offensive and they are not looks I'm going for. But there are times when it can be relevant or even crucial to your writing. If your character is travelling to a part of a country with a strong and well-known dialect, it would be remiss of you to ignore that. Now, a quick prompt is all you need.

Fig 5.1

Good afternoon. Please can you give me a list of ten common dialect words used in Manchester, England. Please include each word in a sentence and explain when it might be used. Thank you.

Good afternoon! Here are ten common dialect words used in Manchester, England, with a sentence and explanation for each:

1. Manc - "I'm a proud Manc." This is short for "Mancunian," which refers to a person from Manchester.
2. Our Kid - "Me and our kid are going to the match." This term is used to refer to a sibling or close friend.
3. Mint - "That new restaurant is mint." This means something is excellent or really good.
4. Barm - "I'll have a bacon barm please." This is short for "barmcake," a type of bread roll commonly eaten in Manchester.
5. Ginnel - "I walked down the ginnel to get to the shops." This is a narrow alleyway between buildings.

6. Mithered - "I'm being mithered by my boss." This means to be pestered or bothered by someone.
7. Batch - "I'm going to put a batch of chips on." This is a term for a quantity of something, usually food.
8. Sound - "That's sound, thanks." This means something is okay or all good.
9. Swerve - "I'm going to swerve that party." This means to avoid something or someone.
10. Bobbins - "That film was bobbin." This means something is rubbish or not very good.

These are just a few examples of the many dialect words used in Manchester, and they can vary depending on the area or community within the city.

I asked for ten, but of course you could ask for more or less. You can specify if there is a particular word you want the dialect for, or even hone it for a specific age range. Let's look at that.

Fig 5.2

Thank you. Are there any phrases that young people from that region would be more likely to use than an older generation?

Yes, there are some phrases that young people from Manchester might be more likely to use than an older generation. Here are some examples:

1. "Sick" or "Sick one" - This is used to describe something that's really cool or impressive. For example, "Did you see that new graffiti art on Stevenson Square? It's sick."
2. "Mood" - This is used to describe a feeling or emotion. For example, "I'm not in the mood for going out tonight."
3. "Dead" - This is used to describe something that's boring or uneventful. For example, "That party was dead, let's go somewhere else."
4. "Lit" - This is used to describe a party or event that's really fun and exciting. For example, "The club last night was lit."
5. "Squad" - This is used to refer to a group of friends or associates. For example, "Me and my squad are going to the game tonight."
6. "YOLO" - This stands for "You Only Live Once" and is used to encourage someone to take a risk or try something new. For example, "Come on, YOLO! Let's go bungee jumping."

These phrases are constantly evolving and changing, and not all young people from Manchester will use them. However, they are examples of slang terms and phrases that are more commonly used by younger generations.

Thank you. Are there any phrases that people over 70 in Manchester might use, that a younger generation may not?

Yes, there are some phrases that people over 70 in Manchester might use that a younger generation may not be as familiar with or use as frequently. Here are some examples:

1. "Gobsmacked" - This is a term used to describe being completely shocked or surprised. For example, "I was absolutely gobsmacked when I heard the news."
2. "Codswallop" - This is a term used to describe something that's nonsense or untrue. For example, "Don't listen to him, it's all codswallop."
3. "Daft as a brush" - This is a phrase used to describe someone who's a bit silly or foolish. For example, "My granddad can be daft as a brush sometimes."
4. "Bobby dazzler" - This is a term used to describe something that's really nice or attractive. For example, "That dress is a real bobby dazzler."
5. "Chuffed" - This is a term used to describe being pleased or happy about something. For example, "I'm absolutely chuffed with my new bike."
6. "Blimey" - This is an exclamation used to express surprise or shock. For example, "Blimey, it's really raining outside."

These phrases may not be as commonly used by younger generations in Manchester, but they are still understood and recognized by many people.

This in my opinion is a great little tool to have. But it's not all there is to this tool. Say you are writing a period romance, and you want to get the tone right. We can ask for help with that too.

While there's nothing completely revolutionary here, it is worth noting, that you can also copy your own dialogue into an AI and it will be able to comment on the authenticity for your chosen time period and location. What I've used in the next example is a piece of text you will see reappear later in the book, but at this point, I've used it solely to comment on how well my work fits with my specified time. Just be warned it doesn't pull any punches.

Fig 5.3

Good afternoon. This text is from my novel. It is set on the silk road in the 14th Century. Can you please assess the writing for authenticity in dialogue and setting:

The four men sat around the table, the drinks untouched. Several times, Ivan cleared his throat as if he were going to start speaking, and the other three men jerked their heads up, eyes forward to look at him, only for the old man to change his mind and return to staring at the table, prompting the others to do the same.

In the end, it was Jack who broke the silence.

"We don't have a choice. We have to do this. We have to hand him over."

"We can't. You know what they'll do to him."

"But that's on him, isn't it? He was the one who chose to steal their supplies."

Silence began to bloom again, but this time it was cut across before it could settle.

"Perhaps we can explain the situation. Explain that his family was starving. He wouldn't have stolen them otherwise."

"Half of their family is probably starving too. And if we don't act, they'll come for us all. We know they will. We don't have enough weapons, supplies, or people, goddamnit, to defend ourselves like that. I just wish he hadn't been so damn stupid. He could've come to one of us."

This time the silence took hold, tension prickling through the air. We had known from the first moment we arrived here what the outcome would be. Now we just had to find the courage to see it through.

The text you've provided is quite engaging and creates a tense atmosphere, which is suitable for a dramatic scenario. However, there are a few anachronisms in the dialogue and setting which detract from the historical authenticity of a story set on the Silk Road in the 14th century:

1. Names: Ivan is a Russian name, which could be plausible depending on the characters' origins, but Jack is more typically English and became popular much later. On the Silk Road, you would be more likely to encounter a variety of Asian, Middle Eastern, and European names. Choosing historically and geographically appropriate names could enhance the authenticity.
2. Dialogue: The use of phrases like "goddamnit" and "damn stupid" are more modern and colloquial, which might not fit the setting of the Silk Road in the 14th century. Consider using more historically accurate expressions or language that would be appropriate for the time period and location.

What's great about this, is not only has it told me what I have done wrong, it has told me how I should improve it. And this leads us wonderfully on to the next chapter.

6. USING AI AS A WRITING TUTOR

For new writers, this has got to be the most important chapter in the book and I debated about putting it first, but I suspected that a lot of people reading this book are not new to writing. Still, I hope this will be of use to everyone in some small way, regardless of where they are in their writing journey.

The first thing any good writing tutor should tell you is to start with the basics. As Stephen King famously said, "If you don't have time to read, you don't have the time (or the tools) to write." Undoubtedly, as authors, we often feel that we're scrambling for time to write and publish our books. However, King's advice still holds true: we need to read, especially within our chosen genre. If you were to attend university, you'd receive a reading list for your course, and the same applies to many writing courses. Now that you're in charge of your own education, ChatGPT can ensure that you're heading in the right direction. Take a look at these two reading lists provided for me, generated based on the prompts I gave it.

Fig 6.1

Good afternoon. I want to write a police procedural novel, set in the East of England. Please can you recommend ten books I read for the last four decades that will provide with with a breadth of material in this genre? Please state the year of publication, where each book is set, and explain why you have chosen it.

Good afternoon! Here are ten police procedural novels set in the East of England that were published in the last four decades that I recommend, with an explanation of why I've chosen each one:

1. "The Last Detective" by Peter Lovesey (1991) - Set in Bath, this book is part of a series featuring Detective Superintendent Peter Diamond. Lovesey is known for his intricate plotting and attention to detail, making his novels a great example of the police procedural genre.
2. "The Crow Trap" by Ann Cleeves (1999) - Set in Northumberland, this is the first book in Cleeves' Vera Stanhope series. Cleeves is known for her well-drawn characters and atmospheric descriptions of the English countryside.
3. "The Seagull" by Ann Cleeves (2017) - Set in Northumberland, this is the eighth book in the Vera Stanhope series. It provides a contemporary perspective of the area while continuing to follow the exploits of the popular character.
4. "In a Dry Season" by Peter Robinson (1999) - Set in Yorkshire, this book is part of the Inspector Banks series. Robinson's writing is known for its strong sense of place and complex characterizations.

5. "The Woodcutter" by Reginald Hill (2010) - Set in Yorkshire, this book is a standalone novel by Hill, who is also known for his Dalziel and Pascoe series. Hill's writing is characterized by its wit, humor, and sharp observations of human behavior.
6. "The Janus Stone" by Elly Griffiths (2010) - Set in Norfolk, this is the second book in Griffiths' Ruth Galloway series. Griffiths' writing is known for its strong sense of place and for weaving together elements of crime fiction and the supernatural.
7. "The Water's Lovely" by Ruth Rendell (2007) - Set in London, this standalone novel by Rendell is a psychological thriller that explores the inner workings of a dysfunctional family. Rendell's work is known for its insightful explorations of human psychology and her skill at creating suspense.
8. "Dead Man's Lane" by Kate Ellis (2020) - Set in Devon, this book is part of the Wesley Peterson series. Ellis is known for her complex plotting and her ability to seamlessly weave together elements of history, mythology, and crime fiction.

9. "Sidney Chambers and the Shadow of Death" by James Runcie (2012) - Set in Cambridge, this book is the first in the Grantchester Mysteries series. Runcie's writing is characterized by its warmth and humor, and by its exploration of issues of faith, morality, and social change.
10. "Murder on the Marshes" by Clare Chase (2018) - Set in Cambridge, this book is the first in the Tara Thorpe series. Chase's writing is known for its intricate plotting and vivid descriptions of the English countryside.

These books were chosen for their strong sense of place, their well-drawn characters, and their skillful use of the conventions of the police procedural genre, and were published in the last four decades.

Although I ask for the last four decades, there is nothing earlier that 1991. I'm sure I could rectify that with a follow up question. Despite that issue, I have a solid range of books to get started on my reading.

Fig 6.2

Thank you. I would also like to write an Urban Fantasy novel where vampire and human societies live integrated. Please can you give me a list of ten books which I should read and why?

Certainly! Here are ten urban fantasy novels that feature vampire and human societies living integrated, with an explanation of why I've chosen each one:

1. "Interview with the Vampire" by Anne Rice - This classic novel is the first book in Rice's Vampire Chronicles series and explores the life of a vampire, Louis de Pointe du Lac, as he tells his story to a human interviewer. It is a seminal work of modern vampire fiction and has had a huge influence on the urban fantasy genre.
2. "Sunshine" by Robin McKinley - This standalone novel is set in a world where vampires are part of society and follows the story of a baker named Sunshine as she becomes entangled in a dangerous vampire plot. It is known for its lush prose and vivid descriptions of both the human and vampire worlds.
3. "The Dresden Files" series by Jim Butcher - This series follows the adventures of Harry Dresden, a wizard and private investigator who often finds himself dealing with supernatural threats. Throughout the series, Dresden encounters various vampires and explores the complex relationship between vampires and humans.

I haven't included the full list, but it has thrown up a really great range of books, and though the communities are not all entirely integrated the way I had asked for, reading the selection is likely to be a solid foundation for anyone getting into this genre.

However, you should know by now that I like to push things further. I don't just want books to read. I want a full creative writing degree structure. So that's what I asked for next.

Fig 6.3

Good evening. I would love to do a creative writing degree, but unfortunately, that route is not available to me. Would you be able to tell me the most common modules taken in such degrees, with the suggested reading list for each module and what I should be analysing each of said modules for?

Good evening! I'd be happy to help you explore the world of creative writing even if you're not able to pursue a degree. Here is a list of common modules typically found in creative writing programs, along with suggested reading lists and what to focus on in each module:

1. Introduction to Creative Writing
   Suggested readings:

- "Bird by Bird" by Anne Lamott
- "On Writing" by Stephen King
- "The Elements of Style" by William Strunk Jr. and E.B. White
  Focus: Develop an understanding of the creative writing process, learn various writing techniques, and explore different forms of creative writing, such as poetry, short stories, and creative nonfiction.

2. Poetry Writing
   Suggested readings:

- "The Poetry Handbook" by Mary Oliver
- "A Poet's Glossary" by Edward Hirsch
- "How to Read a Poem and Fall in Love with Poetry" by Edward Hirsch
  Focus: Understand the structure and form of poetry, learn to employ figurative language and imagery, and experiment with different styles, such as free verse and traditional poetic forms.

3. Fiction Writing
   Suggested readings:

- "Writing Fiction: A Guide to Narrative Craft" by Janet Burroway
- "The Art of Fiction" by John Gardner
- "Aspects of the Novel" by E.M. Forster
  Focus: Learn the elements of fiction, such as character development, plot, setting, dialogue, and theme, and explore different genres, including literary fiction, science fiction, and mystery.

4. Creative Nonfiction Writing
   Suggested readings:

- "The Art of the Personal Essay" by Phillip Lopate
- "The Situation and the Story" by Vivian Gornick
- "Writing Creative Nonfiction" by Carolyn

Believe me, I went to town with this, I asked it to break down the modules further, into lesson structures, with titles, objectives, crib sheets for each of the lectures and commonly given essay titles too. And it provided me with everything I asked for with varying degrees of detail. Including all of that information would have made this book 80% screenshots, so you are just going to have to take my word for it.

However, I can guess what you're thinking. That's all very well and good, but just because you read every book on a degree list, it doesn't mean you're going to be any good at writing. You need to practise the craft and get feedback too.

Before now, feedback predominately came in the form of writing courses or peer groups, either online or in person. Both of these have their advantages and disadvantages. Writing courses can come with extremely experienced tutors, but they can be expensive, particularly those that provide extensive personalised feedback. I know because I paid for enough of them when I started my writing journey. Peer groups might cost nothing in money, but they take away from your time as you are reading and critiquing the other students' work too, and often those critiquing you know no more how to improve your work than you do. Now, however, you have a writing tutor at your fingertips, and honestly, if this is your first novel, I think it would be unwise not to take advantage.

Even if you are experienced, it's interesting to see what feedback it will give you. I offered it a short paragraph with obvious areas that need improvement and asked it to offer me feedback, here's the response I got.

Fig 6.4

Good morning. I have a written a paragraph below as part of my novel. Please can you offer constructive feedback, with areas of strength and weakness and make suggestions on how I could improve? Thank you. "The dead body smelt bad. Flies buzzed around it, and I had to cover my nose so I wasn't sick. This was the first body I had seen and I didn't like it, but it was part of the job I had signed up for. Forcing myself to be brave, I took a deep breath and walked over to the other police officer."

Good morning! Here's my feedback on your paragraph:

Strengths:

- The paragraph is concise and to the point, which is effective in creating a sense of immediacy and urgency.
- The sensory details are vivid and help to immerse the reader in the scene.
- The last sentence sets up a sense of anticipation for what's to come.

Weaknesses:

- The paragraph is a bit too direct and lacks nuance. It would be helpful to provide more context or background information to the reader to help them understand the significance of the dead body and why it's a part of the job.
- The language is simple and could benefit from more variation in sentence structure and word choice.

Suggestions for improvement:

- Consider providing more details about the setting and the circumstances surrounding the discovery of the dead body. This will help to engage the reader and create a more complex and nuanced story.
- Experiment with more complex sentence structures and descriptive language to add depth and complexity to the writing. This will help to create a more immersive reading experience for the reader.
- Consider expanding on the emotions and thoughts of the narrator. This will help to create a more three-dimensional character and add depth to the story.

In this example ChatGPT was able to pick out many of the same things you no doubt spotted about the paragraph, primarily that it wasn't very good.

It has given a list of really valid points on how I could improve my writing while pointing out strengths too. The fact that you know it is a computer and therefore entirely objective in its response, also helps with the feeling of judgement that can often come when people give us negative comments. It's not saying anything to be mean, it's just trying to help you improve, because that's what it was asked to do.

Now what if we want to get a little more specific? The fact that you're reading this book likely implies you've read other writing books or at least researched how to improve your writing skills before now. If that's the case, you've probably come across the phrase "show, don't tell." For those of you who haven't encountered this concept or need a reminder, "show, don't tell" essentially means creating a more immersive experience for readers by showing them the emotions and situations that the characters are going through, rather than just telling the reader how a character is feeling. To put it simply, it's the difference between writing "He was scared as he reached for the handle." and "His hand trembled as he reached for the handle." Good writing is a mixture of showing and telling. But is the computer aware of this and does it know how to improve work? Well the short answer is yes. Take a look.

Fig 6.5

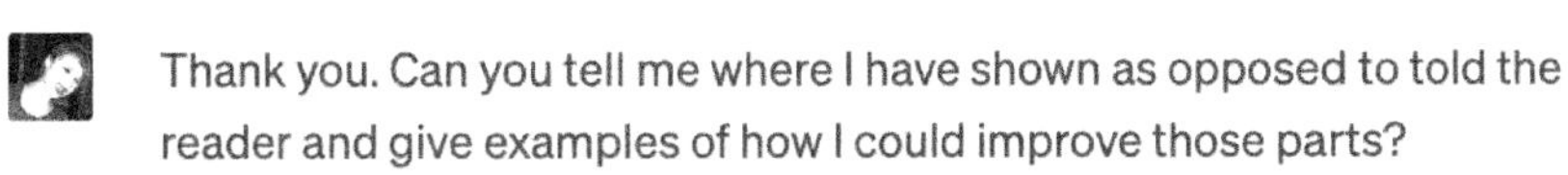

Sure! In your paragraph, you have shown the reader through sensory details like the smell and the buzzing flies, which is great. However, there are still some opportunities to further enhance the showing rather than telling in your writing. Here are some examples of how you could improve those parts:

1. "I had to cover my nose so I wasn't sick."
   Instead of simply telling the reader that the protagonist covered their nose, you could show the physical action by describing how they raised their hand to their face, or how they pinched their nostrils shut to block the smell.
2. "Forcing myself to be brave..."
   While this sentence implies that the protagonist is trying to appear brave, it doesn't show any physical actions or internal thoughts to support this. To improve this, you could describe how the protagonist takes a deep breath to steady their nerves, or include an internal thought such as "I can do this" to show their determination.

3. "I took a deep breath and walked over to the other police officer."
   While this sentence shows the protagonist's physical actions, it doesn't give any insight into their thoughts or emotions. To improve this, you could include an internal thought or dialogue that conveys their thoughts or feelings. For example, "I felt my stomach churn as I took a deep breath and forced myself to approach the other police officer. 'What do we do now?' I asked, my voice shaking."

By incorporating more specific actions, thoughts, and emotions, you can create a more immersive reading experience for the reader and deepen their understanding of the character and the situation.

Not only did ChatGPT recognise the difference between showing and telling, but it also knew how to help improve. That's pretty damn neat. And there was no waiting for a week, panicking on whether my tutor would like my work or not, it was just there. For people who fear putting themselves out there, this could be a fantastic tool. Though, if you are going to write a book, you will mostly likely have to test it with real readers at some point. While ChatGPT might recognise emotional cues, it does not have emotion.

There is no denying that if I were to incorporate ChatGPT's suggestions into my paragraph, the writing would be better, but you still have to write the story. Remember, this is speeding up the writing process, not doing it for you.

So how else can ChatGPT act as our personal writing tutor?

Fig 6.6

Please can you correctly punctate this for me? Let's go for a walk, james said, as he clipped the dogs lead onto his collar. It's a lovely day, we should make the most of it. The dog barked loudly as it bounced up at James legs.

"Let's go for a walk," James said as he clipped the dog's lead onto his collar. "It's a lovely day; we should make the most of it." The dog barked loudly as it bounced up at James' legs.

In this corrected version, I have added a comma after "walk" to indicate that James is speaking. I have also added a comma after "day" and included a semicolon to separate the two independent clauses in the sentence. Finally, I have added an apostrophe to show possession with "James' legs."

Now as well as the corrections it explains, it has also added speech marks too. It's turned what was really a piece of nonsense into something far more legible. As writers we should absolutely be able to do this ourselves, but some people struggle. It could be said that if you need to use ChatGPT to do this for every sentence you write, then maybe a career in writing is not for you, but maybe it is. Maybe you have all the creativity, but don't have that grasp of syntax and grammar that's required to make your work publishable. This could be down to limited education opportunities, or English might not be your first language. If that's the case, then you now have a tool that will enable you to be the storyteller you want to be regardless. Hopefully, over time you would find less and less need to use ChatGPT as you learn the grammatical conventions.

As we all know though, writing isn't just about grammatical correctness, there is far more for authors, new authors in particular, to worry about. Can we get some more generalised writing advice?

Fig 6.7

What are some of the most common mistakes new novelists make in their writing and how can you avoid them?

Writing a novel is a complex and challenging process, and it's natural for new novelists to make mistakes. Here are some common ones and tips on how to avoid them:

1. **Lack of Planning**: Many new novelists start writing without having a clear plan or outline. This often results in plot holes, inconsistencies, and a lack of direction. To avoid this, take the time to outline your novel before you start writing. Establish your main characters, plot, setting, and the major events that will occur.

2. **Overwriting**: New writers often feel the need to describe everything in intricate detail or use overly complex language. However, this can slow down the pace of the novel and bore the reader. To avoid this, focus on using clear, concise language and only include details that are necessary for the plot or character development.
3. **Telling Instead of Showing**: This is a common mistake where the writer tells the reader what's happening instead of showing it through actions, thoughts, senses, and feelings. To avoid this, use vivid language and sensory details to create a picture in the reader's mind.
4. **Flat Characters**: Characters who lack depth or development can fail to engage the reader. Avoid this by ensuring your characters have distinct personalities, flaws, and motivations. Show them growing and changing throughout the story.
5. **Inconsistent Point of View**: It can be confusing for readers if the point of view switches unpredictably. Choose a point of view (first person, third person, etc.) and stick with it unless there's a compelling reason to switch.

Fig 6.8

Good afternoon. I am writing a piece of literary fiction. When editing, what should I do to ensure the work is as tight as possible? Are there certain words I should avoid or sentence starters I don't want to overuse? Thank you.

Good afternoon! Editing is a crucial part of the writing process, and it's great that you're seeking advice on how to tighten your literary fiction. Here are some tips to help you during the editing process:

1. **Trim the Fat**: Cut out any unnecessary words, phrases, or sentences that don't contribute to the plot, character development, or overall theme. This includes redundant or repetitive statements.
2. **Vary Sentence Structure**: Make sure your sentences have variety in length and structure. Too many short sentences can make your writing feel choppy, while too many long sentences can make it difficult to follow. Mixing it up helps maintain the reader's interest.
3. **Avoid Overused Words and Phrases**: Replace clichés, generic descriptions, and overused words (e.g., 'very,' 'just,' 'really,' 'suddenly') with more specific and vivid language. Use a thesaurus to find alternatives, but ensure they fit the tone and context of your story.
4. **Watch for Filter Words**: Filter words are unnecessary words that distance the reader from the character's experience. Examples include 'she saw,' 'he felt,' or 'they noticed.' Remove these words and describe the experience directly.

Even for seasoned writers these are solid pieces of writing advice and hopefully following them is going to mean we are producing better books.

I know some of you will be thinking these are just generic points you can get off the internet. However, the key and the beauty with using ChatGPT as a writing tutor is that you can tailor it entirely to your needs and writing ability. If you know you need to add more sensory description in your writing, give it a paragraph and ask for advice on where you could add that detail. If you struggle with run on sentences, ask it how you could structure your sentences better. Of course, you could put your writing into an AI and simply ask it to add those things for you, but then that's not using AI as a writing tutor, that's using it to try to do the job for you, and to be honest, you're probably going to be disappointed with the results. Either that, or your readers will be.

Still, used ethically, this is one of the most powerful tools available to help develop you and your writing.

7. USING AI IN MARKETING

If you are a self-published author then you will likely be handling your own marketing. This aspect of the writing business is so often a nemesis to many writers. Well fear not,

AI can help you fine tune marketing material and give you the best shot at selling your books.

So how can AI help you? There's a lot to unpack here, so let's start at the one thing all writers will need. Blurbs.

How many of you out there would rather write an 80,000 word novel than a 250 word blurb? Sometimes it feels impossible to encapsulate everything that we have created over the previous months, if not years, into this tiny snapshot and yet it is required for every book we do. So why not take some of the pain out if at let AI have a go? While it probably won't be perfect what it will do is give you a strong starting point.

Fig 7.1

Good afternoon. I have a plot for a story, that I would like you to make a blurb for. It is a fantasy booked aimed at young adults. He is a summary. The Fay king has been murdered at night in his sleep, and people assume the humans are to blame. They are all rounded up at night, but some of them run away and escape. One of the ones who runs away is a human girl called Del. She is the only one of her family who escapes and is determined to free them. Em is a Fay prince who thinks it is someone in the palace responsible for the kings death and wants to find the truth. Thank you.

In a world where tensions run high between the human and Fay kingdoms, the unexpected murder of the Fay king ignites a dangerous blame game. Humans are accused and rounded up in the dead of night, leaving families torn apart and innocent lives at risk. Del, a human girl, is forced to flee and is determined to find a way to free her family from captivity. Meanwhile, Em, a Fay prince, suspects that the killer is someone within the palace and is determined to uncover the truth. As Del and Em's paths cross, they realize they must put their differences aside and work together to uncover the real culprit before more innocent lives are lost. But with secrets and danger lurking at every turn, can they succeed before it's too late? A thrilling fantasy adventure for young adults, filled with magic, mystery, and a race against time to save two kingdoms.

First, I want to address how the information I gave it was weak. That was deliberate. I wanted to know what it would be able do with limited details to go on, and the truth is, it did a fairly good job. It's got a hook, it's added intrigue. I don't think it's too horrendous. Of course, the more specifics you can add to it, the more you can hone it to what you are after.

AI is fantastic for anything that has a short word limit, such as ad copy, hooks, promo lines, though be warned it won't always stick to the word count exactly, so don't assume it has. Carrying on from the blurb it gave me, I asked it for some ten-word hooks, but you can see it was rather loose with that word count. Specifying for a second time, normally makes it take more notice, though I'm going to save the screenshots on that one.

Fig 7.2

Thank you. Please can you write a selection of 10 word hooks for this story? Thank you.

1. A Fay king is murdered, and humans are blamed.
2. Del is the only one of her family to escape.
3. Em, a Fay prince, is determined to find the truth.
4. Tensions run high between the human and Fay kingdoms.
5. Secrets and danger lurk at every turn.
6. Can Del and Em put their differences aside?
7. A race against time to save two kingdoms.
8. Magic and mystery intertwine in this fantasy adventure.
9. Innocent lives are at risk, and time is running out.
10. The truth must be uncovered before it's too late.

Now, what other parts of book marketing can ChatGPT help us with? By this point in the book it shouldn't surprise you that the easiest thing to do is ask. As I've already said, ChatGPT was designed to chat, so give it that opportunity.

Fig 7.3

Good morning, I'm a novelist and I need to improve my marketing skills. What are some ways that ChatGPT can help me with the marketing of my book? Thank you.

Good morning! I'm happy to help you with marketing your book. Here are some ways ChatGPT can assist you:

1. Crafting a compelling book description: ChatGPT can help you write a captivating book description that highlights the most engaging aspects of your story and entices potential readers.
2. Creating engaging social media content: ChatGPT can generate ideas for social media posts to promote your book, as well as help you draft the content itself, including captions, hashtags, and calls to action.
3. Blogging and guest posts: ChatGPT can help you generate ideas for blog posts related to your book or its themes. It can also assist with writing the content, which can be shared on your own blog or submitted as guest posts to relevant websites.
4. Email marketing: ChatGPT can help you draft engaging newsletters, updates, and promotional emails to send to your mailing list, keeping your readers informed and excited about your book.
5. Author bio and press releases: ChatGPT can help you write a compelling author bio and draft press releases to promote your book to media outlets, bookstores, and other relevant platforms.

6. Identifying target audience and marketing strategies: ChatGPT can help you identify your target audience and suggest marketing strategies specifically tailored to reach them.
7. Crafting ad copy: ChatGPT can help you create effective and engaging ad copy for various advertising platforms such as Facebook, Instagram, Google Ads, and Amazon Advertising.
8. Brainstorming promotional ideas: ChatGPT can generate a list of promotional ideas, such as contests, giveaways, collaborations with influencers, or special edition releases, to create buzz around your book.
9. Answering reader questions: ChatGPT can help you interact with readers by answering questions about your book, your writing process, or any other relevant topics.
10. Networking: ChatGPT can provide guidance on how to build relationships with other authors, bloggers, and influencers in your genre or industry, helping you create a strong network of support.

Remember to always double-check and edit any content generated by ChatGPT to ensure it aligns with your voice and marketing goals. Good luck with your book marketing journey!

This is a pretty comprehensive list and even if you're not going to use ChatGPT to help craft any of them, it's useful to remember there are all these options available to you to promote your books.

Many of these are self-explanatory. I'm know that I can ask ChatGPT to give me ten possible blog topics to talk about that are in some way linked to my books and it will manage it, but now I want to look at some of them a little more closely. I'm intrigued to know how ChatGPT can help with networking, so let's see what it gives me.

Fig 7.4

This is great thank you. I really want to be better at networking. How would you suggest I do this?

Improving your networking skills is essential for building relationships and expanding your reach as an author. Here are some suggestions on how to become better at networking:

1. Attend events: Participate in writing conferences, workshops, book fairs, and literary festivals. These events provide opportunities to meet fellow authors, agents, publishers, and industry professionals. Be prepared with your elevator pitch, business cards, and a positive attitude.
2. Join online communities: Engage with writing groups, forums, and social media communities related to your genre or industry. Participate in discussions, offer advice, and share your experiences. This can help you build relationships with like-minded individuals.
3. Collaborate with others: Seek out opportunities to collaborate with other authors, bloggers, or influencers in your genre. This can include co-writing projects, guest posts, interviews, or social media takeovers.
4. Engage on social media: Be active on platforms like Twitter, Instagram, Facebook, and LinkedIn. Follow and engage with authors, publishers, agents, and book enthusiasts. Share your thoughts, ask questions, and comment on others' posts.

Okay, so it's not helping us network, but rather giving us a guide on how to network effectively. It's got some valid points, but nothing ground-breaking. What about exploring one of the other ideas it gives in more detail.

Fig 7.5

Thank you. Can you please suggest some places I could find collaboration opportunities?

Certainly! Collaboration opportunities can be found in various places, both online and offline. Here are some suggestions for finding potential collaborators:

1. Social media platforms: Follow and engage with other authors, bloggers, and influencers in your genre on platforms like Twitter, Instagram, Facebook, and LinkedIn. Look for collaboration opportunities in their posts or reach out directly with a proposal.
2. Online forums and communities: Join writing communities, discussion boards, or Facebook groups related to your genre or niche. These platforms often have dedicated threads or sections for collaboration requests, or you can start a new discussion to express your interest.
3. Writing conferences and events: Attend writing conferences, workshops, book fairs, and literary festivals. Use these opportunities to network with other writers and industry professionals who may be interested in collaborating.
4. Local writing groups or meetups: Find local writing groups or meetups in your area using platforms like Meetup.com or through community centers and libraries. These groups often have members who are interested in collaboration.

Once again, it's not actually offering anything in the way of real places to find these opportunities. That's not surprising, because ChatGPT only has access to information available up to 2021 and can offer nothing in real time. That means if you are asking for anything, be it for marketing or research purposes that happened later than that, you are going to be out of luck. However, as I will explore shortly, the prompt you give the AI dictates entirely the type of response you will be given and a little bit of tweaking means we can still use ChatGPT to provide us with something useful.

Fig 7.6

Good morning. I am looking for places to publishing my short Science Fiction stories online. Can you suggest any?

Good morning! There are several online platforms and magazines that accept and publish short science fiction stories. Here's a list of some notable options to consider:

1. Clarkesworld Magazine (**http://clarkesworldmagazine.com/**): A Hugo and World Fantasy Award-winning publication that publishes a variety of speculative fiction, including science fiction.
2. Asimov's Science Fiction (**https://www.asimovs.com/**): A highly respected magazine featuring science fiction short stories, novellas, and poetry. Named after the renowned author Isaac Asimov.
3. Apex Magazine (**https://apex-magazine.com/**): A genre-bending publication that features science fiction, fantasy, and horror stories.
4. Lightspeed Magazine (**http://www.lightspeedmagazine.com/**): A highly acclaimed online publication that focuses on science fiction and fantasy short stories.

The list in Fig 7.6 goes on to offer another six publications. Still, you might well be thinking that a Google search will give us pretty much the same results as ChatGPT. Once again it is the prompts we use that make the difference. Adding a couple of extra words, will increase the output greatly as you can see.

Fig 7.7

Thank you. Can you please give me 100 places where I could submit a short story and give the grenres they accept? Thank you

Here is a list of 100 places to submit your short stories, along with the genres they accept. Remember to review each platform's submission guidelines and requirements before submitting your work.

1. Clarkesworld Magazine (Science Fiction, Fantasy): http://clarkesworldmagazine.com/
2. Asimov's Science Fiction (Science Fiction): https://www.asimovs.com/
3. Apex Magazine (Science Fiction, Fantasy, Horror): https://apex-magazine.com/
4. Lightspeed Magazine (Science Fiction, Fantasy): http://www.lightspeedmagazine.com/
5. Strange Horizons (Speculative Fiction): http://strangehorizons.com/
6. Daily Science Fiction (Science Fiction, Fantasy): https://dailysciencefiction.com/
7. Tor.com (Science Fiction, Fantasy): https://www.tor.com/
8. InterGalactic Medicine Show (Science Fiction, Fantasy): http://www.intergalacticmedicineshow.com/

An important disclaimer here. Because ChatGPT does not have access to real time information, some of these websites might no longer be live and it can't help you if you are after the latest information, but we will come to a possible solution for this and also a few more tools to help with our marketing, but for that, we need to move away from ChatGPT and look at alternative AI tools available. Finally it is worth noting that all those links are live if you are in ChatCPT.

8. SUDOWRITE

Alternative AI software for writing

In this book all these examples I have given have been using ChatGPT with either GPT-3.5 or GPT-4 as the AI used, but in this chapter I will talk through a couple of other programs out there, highlighting some of the benefits you might find from using these. As I promised in the previous topic we will look a little more at marketing, and real-time feedback, but first we are going to stick with writing.

Sudowrite

As the name would suggest, this has clearly been designed for writers, one look at the homepage and you can see that. It can help you brainstorm, re-write or add descriptions based solely on the senses you want to include.

Fig 8.1

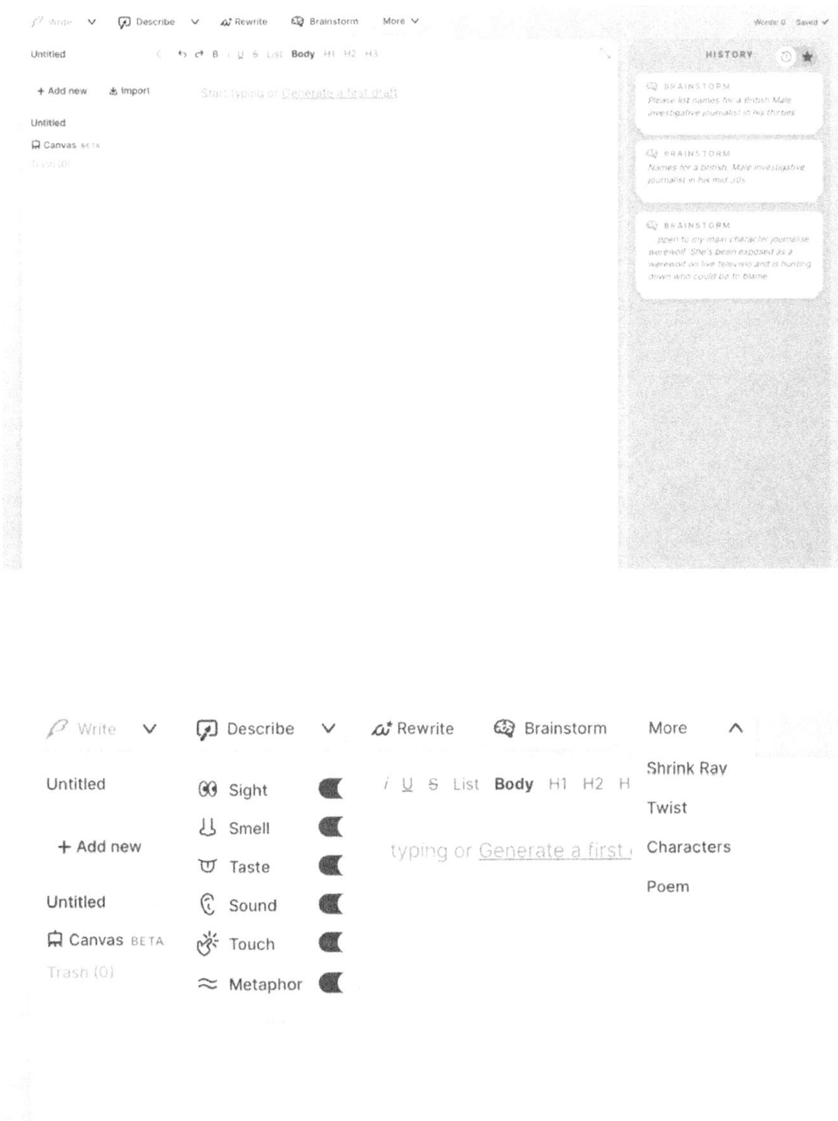

So, let's have a go. I want a description for a living room filled with cats. Once I select that sentence, and hit describe it gives me a selection of possible descriptions, all categorised into sight, smell, taste, etc. If I don't like them, I can click *describe* again and it will spit out a chunk of new possible descriptions for me.

Fig 8.2

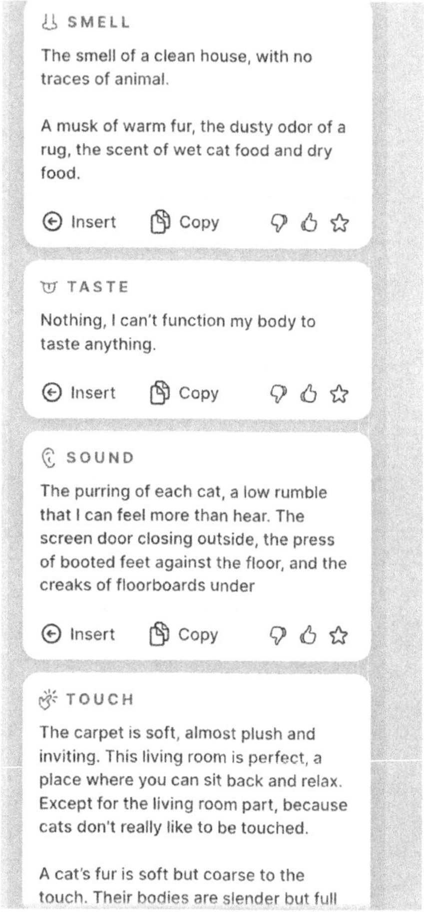

It's fun, and like ChatGPT it's likely to get your thoughts whirring with other ideas, even if you're not going to take any of the exact descriptions it's given you. It's a slightly more colourful interface and easy to use, so it's not surprising that this is a popular option among writers.

Now let's have a look at one of the other functions which is popular. To use these functions, you have to have a minimum of twenty words already written, so that is what I did. I wrote a fairly mundane couple of sentences for it to work with.

Two men are waiting in the rain at the train station. One is dressed in ripped jeans with a hoodie over his head while the other is in a business suit and has a large black umbrella to protect him.

It might look incredibly dull and badly written — okay, it is dull and badly written, but Sudowrite can do a lot with this. The first thing we can get it to do is rewrite and the way the program has been set up, there is no need for prompts you simply click the rewrite button. Then you can select what kind of re-write you want it to do, from making it more descriptive, to ensuring you are showing and not telling or even adding more inner conflict.

Fig 8.3

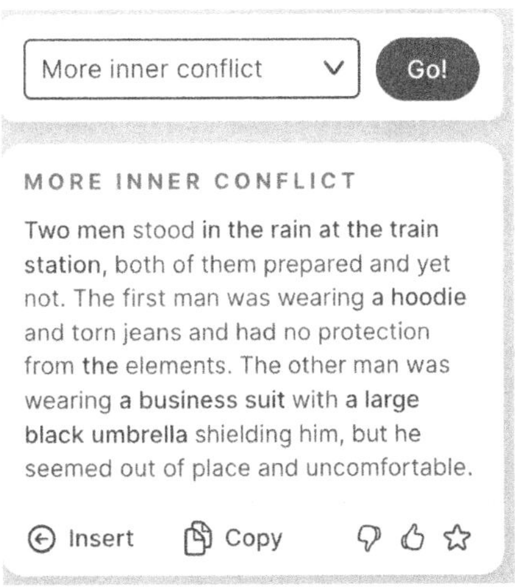

What I like about this, is how it shows you what it is changing. If you want to improve as a writer, this is such an important thing to be able to see. The same with the Show not Tell.

Fig 8.4

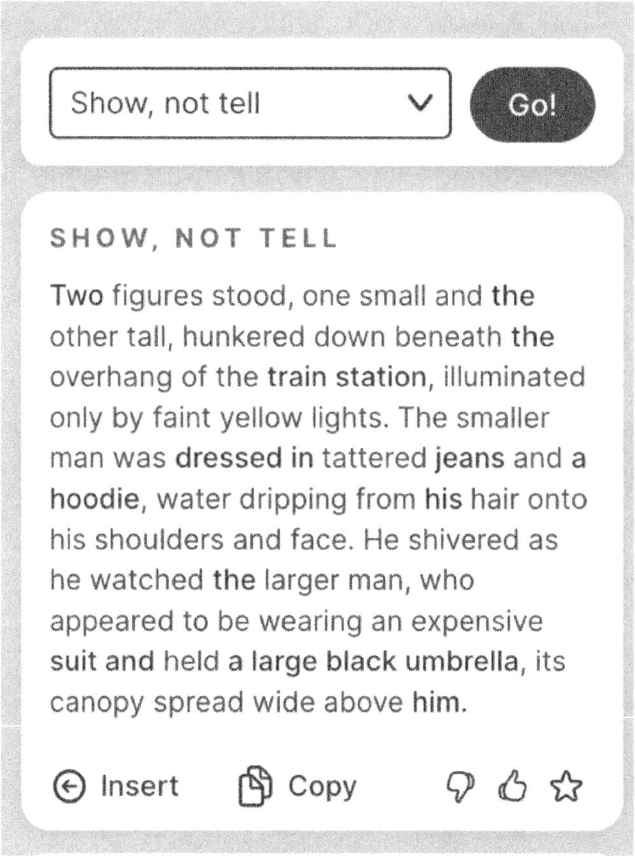

In this particular example it doesn't mention rain at all, it is all implied, which again, is a great lesson for a new writer to learn.

If rather than clicking on describe, we click **write,** then Sudowrite gives me this list of options.

Fig 8.5

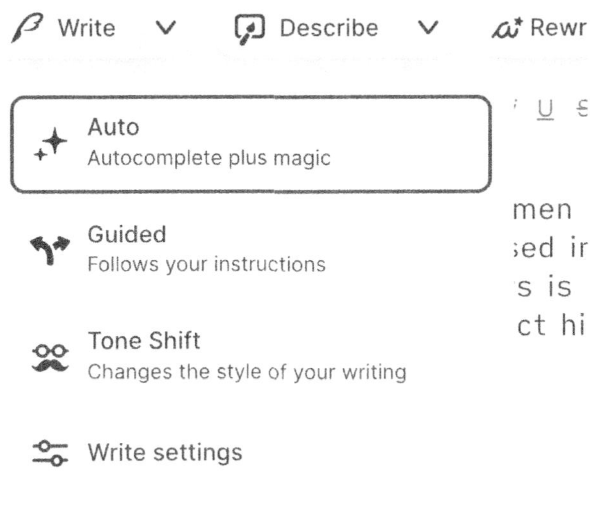

It will carry on writing my story for me, even though I only had to give it twenty words to get started. I selected the auto option and this is what it gave me.

Fig 8.6

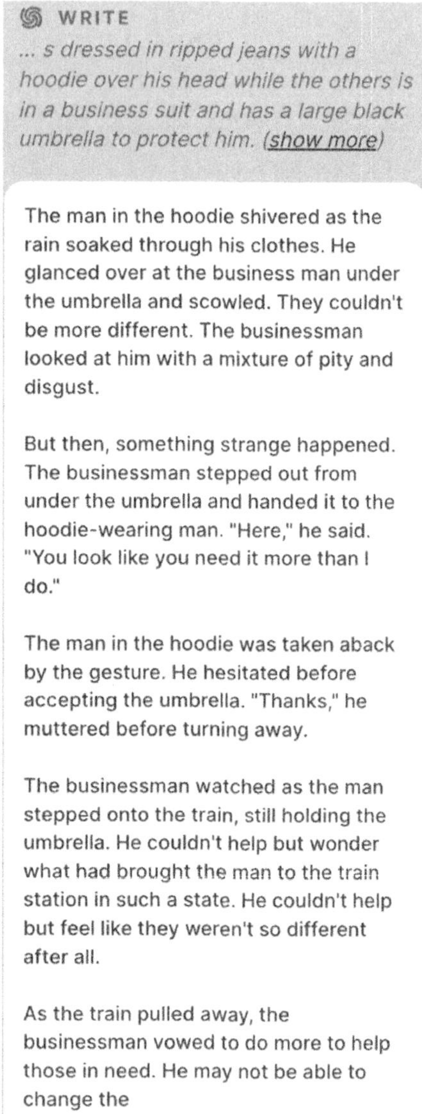

WRITE

... s dressed in ripped jeans with a hoodie over his head while the others is in a business suit and has a large black umbrella to protect him. (show more)

The man in the hoodie shivered as the rain soaked through his clothes. He glanced over at the business man under the umbrella and scowled. They couldn't be more different. The businessman looked at him with a mixture of pity and disgust.

But then, something strange happened. The businessman stepped out from under the umbrella and handed it to the hoodie-wearing man. "Here," he said. "You look like you need it more than I do."

The man in the hoodie was taken aback by the gesture. He hesitated before accepting the umbrella. "Thanks," he muttered before turning away.

The businessman watched as the man stepped onto the train, still holding the umbrella. He couldn't help but wonder what had brought the man to the train station in such a state. He couldn't help but feel like they weren't so different after all.

As the train pulled away, the businessman vowed to do more to help those in need. He may not be able to change the

As I gave it no indication of how I wanted the story to go, it continued it on in its chosen manner. I can however specify what I want to happen, by selecting the **guided** option, which is what I'm going to do this time. This is the prompt I gave it.

The two men are spies and have to exchange secret information without arousing suspicion.

Fig 8.7

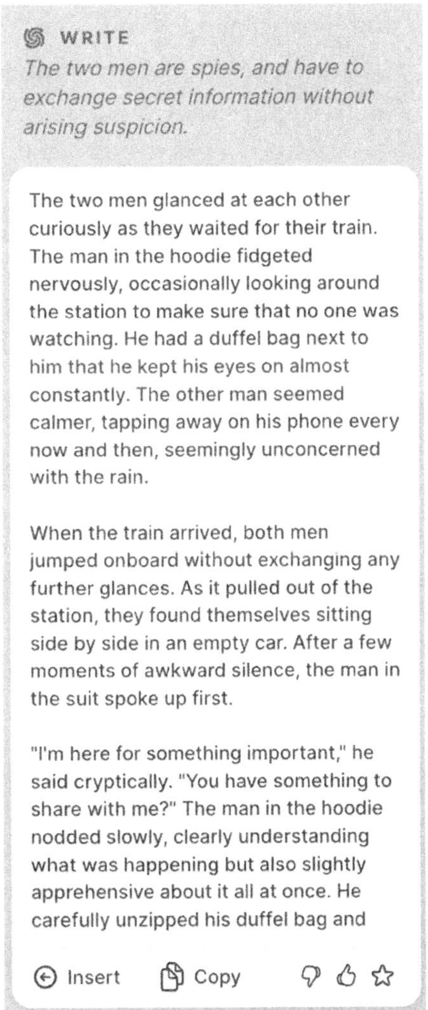

Often I find with writing, that seeing what you don't want, can help prompt what you do, and I think this is great for that. I don't want stilted dialogue, perhaps I didn't want any at all, and seeing that down there, confirms it for me. It also gives me knew points to consider as I'm writing. Are they both getting on the train? Are they going to sit opposite one another, or will one simply drop off the item and go? Just like ChatGPT this offers you a sounding board to bounce ideas off, and with that in mind, I'm going to show you another function on SudoWrite. The brainstorm. It's exactly what it says, a platform to help you consider various options and it looks like this.

Fig 8.8

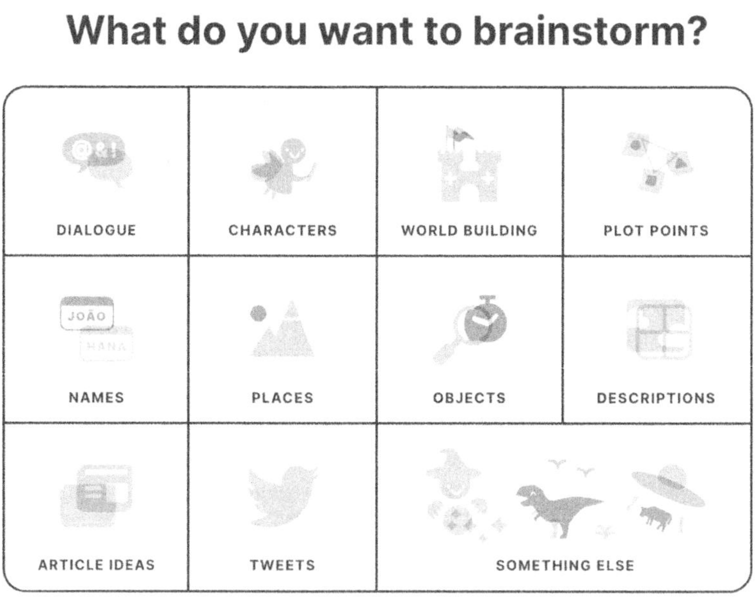

Let's have a look at what it can do for places. This is the first thing I see, and I've filled it in with a few details, though I left the examples blank, as I don't know any. (Or I want it to think that I don't.) Adding that extra info to the context though, really helps.

Fig 8.9

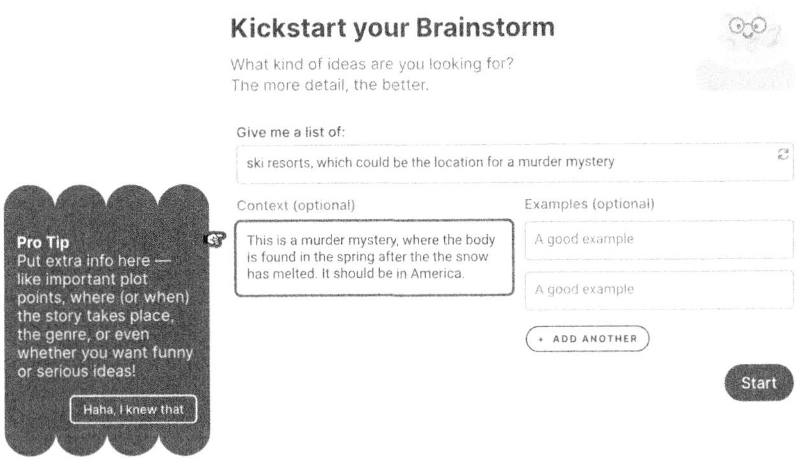

Let's see what it's gives me as suggestions.

Fig 8.10

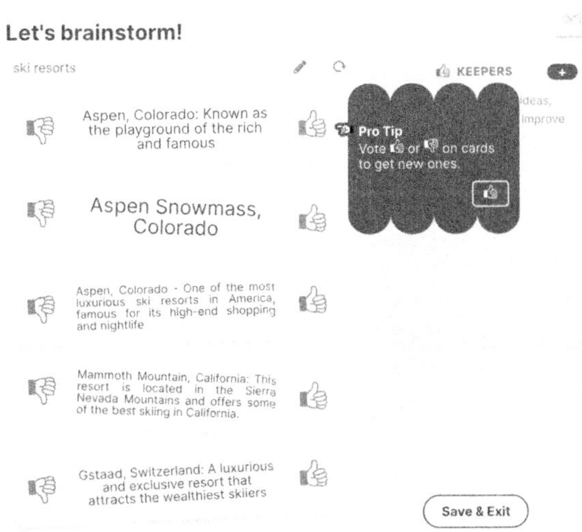

These are good suggestions, which I can accept or reject, a bit like speed dating for writing and after I've dismissed or accepted an idea, it gives me another based on the feedback. Now, thanks to Sudowrite, I have a great place to start my ski-slope murder mystery. In my opinion this is as close as you can get to bouncing ideas off another person and demonstrates and how AI can really benefit authors. As you saw from the Fig 8.8, there are lots of different things Sudowrite can help you brainstorm, but it also has another feature in the Beta stage; Canvas which allows you to brainstorm in a far more visual manner.

This option is available in the paid Sudowrite only, and many people might not find it necessary, but given that it is there, I thought I'd share with you. (Don't worry if you can't read the text, I just wanted you to see the style.)

Fig 8.11

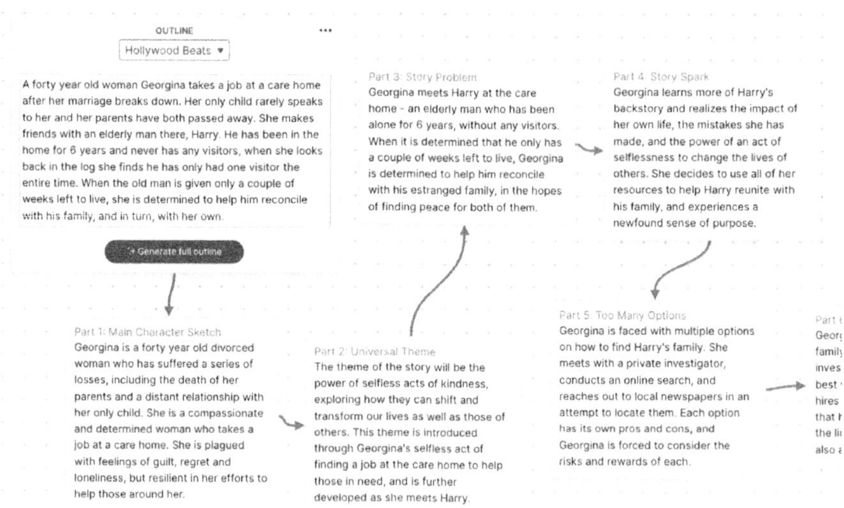

Like all of Sudowrite, this is fairly intuitive to use. I placed a quick plot in the generator selecting the option of Hollywood Beats as my generation option. I could have also chosen others including Hero's Journey and Romance Story. Now rather than just a stream of text or bullet points, you get these little cards which have been deliberately generated to try to match the key points of its Hollywood Beats outline.

There are some interesting points in brings to life here, like the need for the theme to be running through the story, or the addition of extra characters because it doesn't (rightly or wrongly) believe that two characters are enough to tell this story.

Now if we look at some the points we can see that despite these additions, not much improvement has been made on the plot, and it is still up to me, to add all of the actual details and events, just like it was in ChatGPT. Given that they are using the same AI, it is not surprising.

Fig 8.12

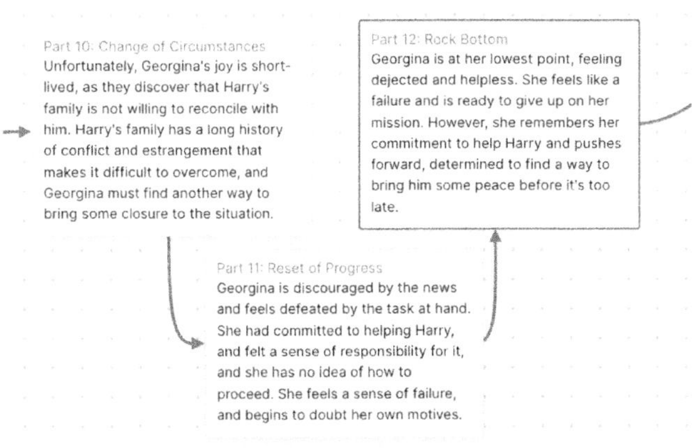

One thing that is useful is how it comes up with other options, just like in the previous format, that you can swap into your plot if you don't like the one you been give.

Fig 8.13

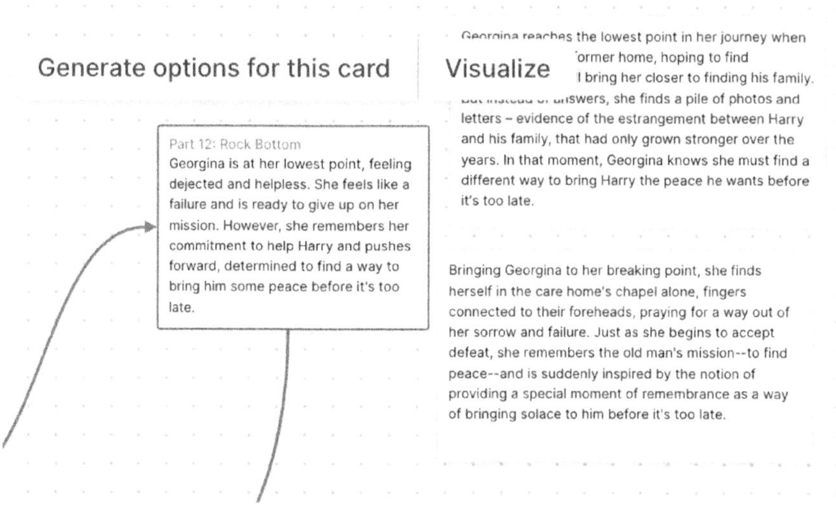

Again, nothing earth shattering but the whole point that I have been trying to make through this, is the power of AI as a sounding board. Seeing wrong options that helps you lead to the right one.

This version of it has another tool embedded into it. This feature comes with premium accounts, and it is able to generate images from your text.

Fig 8.14

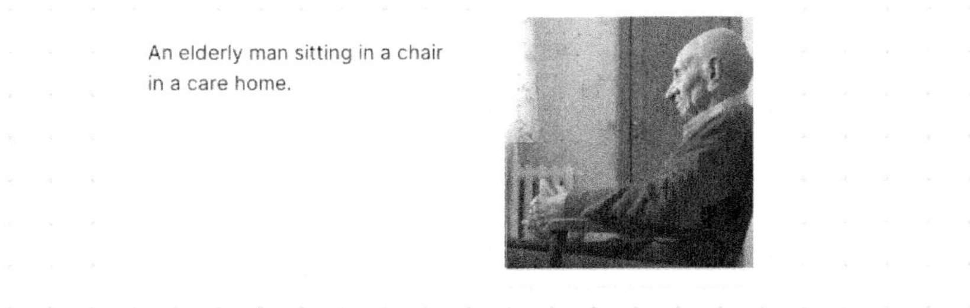

There are those people who do like visual representation for their characters and settings, as well as those who like to keep a variety of ideas gathered together in one place, and for those people I think this could be an excellent option.

9. WRITESONIC

JUST AS THE NAME SUGGESTS, WRITESONIC IS ABOUT HELPING YOU write fast, and is geared up for all genres of writing. The instant you log on, you are faced with a plethora of options from Ads and Marking to Social Media and Website Copy. There is a lot to get your head around.

Fig 9.1

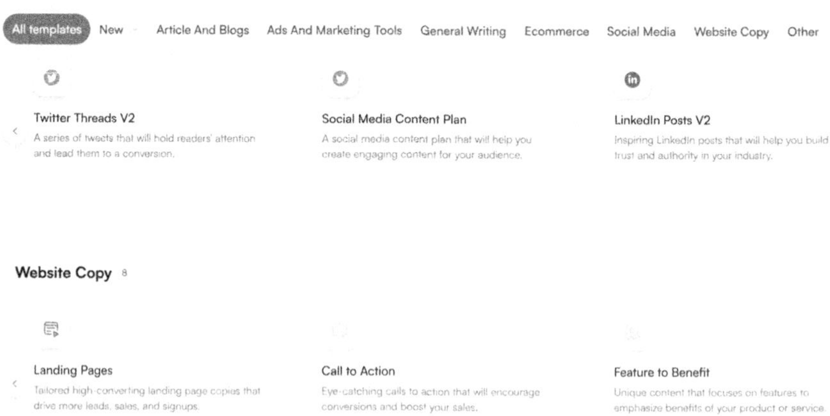

It uses the same GPT-3.5 and GPT-4 technology, as ChatGPT and Sudowrite, but the way it has been set up is more like Sudowrite, in that the prompts are determined by what you have selected it to do.

Given my job, I clicked on Stories.

Fig 9.2

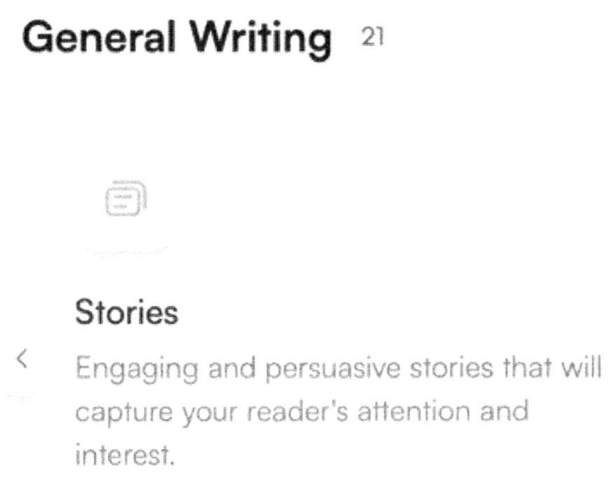

Now, I want to be as transparent as possible in this book, which is why I'm telling you that what you see here, is the very first thing I asked Writesonic to do for me. I am learning about this programme in real time with you, so though I am familiar with ChatGPT, for example, the prompts it likes and have some vague idea what to expect as its output, I had no idea what to expect the first time I used Writesonic.

Deciding to keep things on an even footing, I used that same brief summary I had for Sudowrite and asked for plot.

I want to give the negatives first.

You are limited to 600 characters. I struggled with that. Particularly as the first three times I tried to run it, I did not put any prompt in the box, assuming it was not needed, and it would not load a response. This meant I had to cut into my character count even further to ask it to write the opening paragraphs. That was irritating, but here is what I put in the end. You can see I used every character there was!

Fig 9.3

Description * 600 / 600

Write four paragraphs for when the lead character arrives at the home for the 1st time A forty year old woman Georgina takes a job at a care home after her marriage breaks down. Her only child rarely speaks to her and her parents have both passed away. She makes friends with an elderly man there, Harry. He has been in the home for 6 years and never has any visitors, when she looks back in the log she finds he has only had one visitor the entire time. When the old man is given only a couple of weeks left to live, she is determined to help him reconcile with his family, and in turn, with her own

Tone Of Voice 7 / 100

Emotive

Now, what it showed me is immense. But I'm not entirely sure that's a good thing. First let me show you.

Fig 9.4

Georgina's heart raced with anxiety as she pulled up to the care home. She had always been intimidated by the thought of entering a facility full of elderly people. But her recent situation had left her with no choice and she was now in desperate need of a job. With a deep breath, she walked through the doors and was greeted by the stale aroma of disinfectant and aging bodies.

As she began to settle into her new role, Georgina met Harry. He was a quiet, gentle soul who seemed content with his solitary existence. However, something about him spoke to her on a deeper level. They shared stories, laughed, and cried together. One afternoon, Georgina discovered something in the logbook that changed everything.

Harry had been in the care home for six years and only had one visit from his family. Georgina couldn't help but feel heartbroken for him. She realized that he deserved better, that everyone deserves better. When Harry was given a bleak prognosis, she knew that she had to do everything in her power to help him reconcile with his family, and maybe even her own.

With each passing day, Georgina worked tirelessly to locate Harry's estranged family. She dug through old records, made countless phone calls, and wrote letters. Finally, she managed to track them down. When Harry's family showed up in the care home, they were shocked to see the transformation in him. He was glowing with joy and happiness, surrounded by love and affection.

Georgina watched from the corner as Harry hugged his family. Tears streamed down her face and she realized that this was what life was all about. She left work that day feeling fulfilled and amazed at the power of love and connection. Months passed and Georgina became a permanent fixture in Harry's life. When he eventually passed away, her heart was heavy, knowing that she had made a difference in his life. And in turn, Harry had helped her reconcile with her own family, healing wounds that had been festering for years.

347 words / 1636 characters

There is so much information here. From my 600 characters it gave me four variations of the previous example, totalling around 1400 words. But how much use is it? I specified those introductory paragraphs, but instead, what it has tried to do is give me an entire story.

With so much here, I personally feel I would spend far too long wading through this to perhaps find a phrase I might integrate.

This time, as you can see, I cut down my character count by a lot, and included more prompts the way I would with ChatGPT.

Fig 9.5

Description * 168 / 600

Write four paragraphs for when the lead character arrives at a care home, to start a new job after her marriage has broken down. Please ensure a feeling of despondency.

I have only posted one response again, although this time it gave me six variations, totally 2000 words.

Fig 9.6

As Alice approached the care home, her heart sank. This was not where she wanted to be. She had hoped for so much more from life, but here she was, starting a new job after her marriage had broken down. She felt a deep sense of despondency, like she was trapped in a life she never wanted.

The care home was an imposing building, with large, white windows, and an austere facade. Alice had never worked in a care home before, and she didn't know what to expect. As she walked through the entrance, she felt the weight of the world on her shoulders. She was alone, with no support, no friends, and no family, just the four walls that surrounded her.

As she made her way down the corridor, Alice could hear the sound of quiet voices, the shuffling of feet, and the occasional laughter. The atmosphere was peaceful, but it did little to soothe her despondency. Alice came across a group of people sitting in the communal living area. Their faces brightened as she approached, and they greeted her with warm smiles and kind words.

Alice felt a glimmer of hope as she realized that this new job might not be so bad after all. Perhaps she could find a sense of purpose here, a reason to keep going. As she sat down and began to talk to the residents, she started to feel a spark of joy in her heart. This was not the end for her, but a new beginning.

This is much more useful, has several nice turns of phrase. It's got that air of solemnity I asked for. Could I paste it straight into a novel? In my opinion, not if we want it to be enjoyed by our readers. Nice turns of phrase are not enough to create a compelling story, and I think this example shows that really nicely. It's a bit like those chapter headings we got when we were looking at plots. Nice in theory, but really not as beneficial as you might first think. There is no dialogue, no sense of pace that a writer would be able to control and by the fourth paragraph it's already rushed to weeks ahead. But you can certainly use it to knock out some ideas.

Given all the other features of Writesonic, I think it's fair to have a look at a couple of those too before we finish the chapter. Time to turn our attention to marketing. Writesonic is set up for marketing, from Facebook ads to Instagram comments and a whole heap of other things there too.

I decided to write an ad for a new horror book. When I open up the page I want, one aspect that jumps out at me straight away is that I can only use American English. Other languages are an option, but British English, is not one of them. This probably can likely be solved with a prompt, but it seems like a bizarre omission.

Right, let's see what it has given us. For this I chose the Facebook Ads option in the main menu.

Fig 9.7

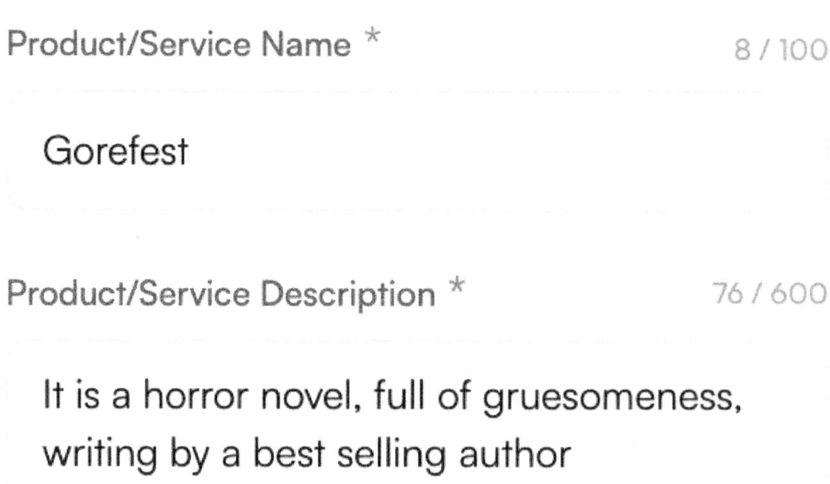

Opt. 1

Image Copy:
Design Idea: A blood-spattered cover with a haunting image of a ghostly figure lurking in the background.
Tagline: "Dare to read the ultimate horror experience? Gorefest is here!"

Text Copy:
Attention horror fans! Brace yourself for the most terrifying journey of your life! Gorefest, the bone-chilling novel by a bestselling author, is finally here! Packed with gruesome scenes and bone-chilling plot twists, this book is not for the faint-hearted. Get ready to be scared out of your wits!

On this release day, indulge in the ultimate horror experience with Gorefest. Be the first among your friends to get your hands on this spine-tingling novel. Order now to experience the most immersive and terrifying journey of your life.

Don't miss out on this once-in-a-lifetime opportunity to feed your horror addiction. Click the link to order Gorefest today!

Once again, five options were provided, of which I have shown the first, and I think there are some useful elements here. It suggests images to use, gives taglines and always includes a call to action. If, like many of us, you find it easier to write a full chapter, than a call to action, I think this is a fantastic tool to have, particularly to help build your confidence in ensuring your ads have everything they need. There is no denying that Writesonic and Sudowrite have some excellent alternatives for those who perhaps do not like the chatbot format of ChatGPT. But for those that do, I have one more to show you.

10. GOOGLE BARD, MICROSOFT BING, AMAZON BEDROCK

Now forgive me if I go on a bit here, I've got a fair bit to unpack. The first thing to acknowledge is that Google Bard is like ChatGPT, a chatbot, meaning you type away and get your response. So does that mean it's the same? Not according to Bard! This is the response I got when I asked it.

Fig 10.1

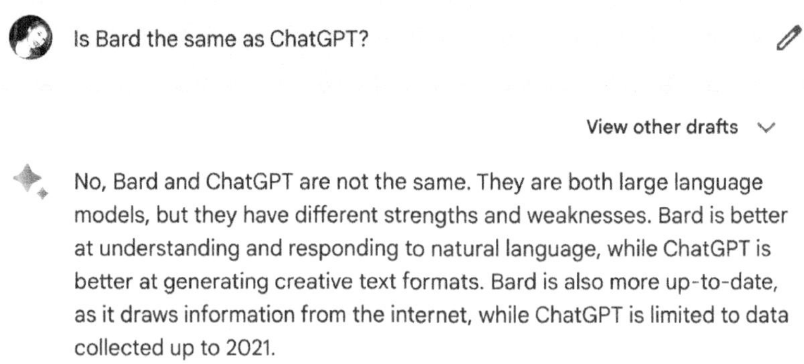

Here is a table that summarizes the key differences between Bard and ChatGPT:

Feature	Bard	ChatGPT
Data source	Internet	2021 data
Strengths	Natural language understanding, up-to-date information	Creative text generation
Weaknesses	Can be inaccurate, limited to text functions	Needs careful prompting to generate more detailed responses

Ultimately, the best language model for you will depend on your specific needs. If you need a model that can understand and respond to natural language, Bard is a good choice. If you need a model that can generate creative text formats, ChatGPT is a good choice.

I think it feels quite strongly about these differences! Joking aside, this does summarise the difference nicely. You will also see that it has the reference to where it has found the information from at a link in the bottom. This is more important than it might first appear, because it tells you where you can verify the information – something we know is necessary given AI's occasional issues with getting things wrong. Now the other extremely important difference to consider here is that unlike GPT-3.5 and GPT4, which only have data up until 2021, Google Bard has access to the internet and therefore real time data. This could be a hugely powerful tool. I say *could be*, because Google Bard is, at the time of writing this, still in development and there are a few kinks that still need to be ironed out.

Nevertheless, let's dive in and see what it can do.

Fig 10.2

If I was to ask you to write a plot for a cozy mystery novel, what information would you need me to give you first?

View other drafts

If you were to ask me to write a plot for a cozy mystery novel, I would need you to give me the following information first:

- The setting of the novel: This could be a small town, a village, or even a city. The setting should be somewhere that the reader can easily visualize and feel comfortable in.
- The protagonist of the novel: This is the character who will be solving the mystery. The protagonist should be someone that the reader can relate to and root for.
- The antagonist of the novel: This is the character who committed the murder. The antagonist should be someone that the reader can both fear and hate.
- The murder itself: This is the event that sets the plot in motion. The murder should be something that is both shocking and believable.
- The clues: These are the things that the protagonist will use to solve the mystery. The clues should be both obvious and hidden, and they should lead the protagonist down a winding path to the truth.
- The solution to the mystery: This is the big reveal at the end of the novel. The solution should be satisfying and believable, and it should leave the reader feeling satisfied.

Once I have this information, I can start brainstorming ideas for the plot. I will use my knowledge of cozy mysteries to create a story that is both exciting and suspenseful. I will also make sure that the story is full of likable characters and clever clues. With your help, I can create a cozy mystery novel that readers will love.

Straightaway we can see it's very similar to ChatGPT, though it does add alternative answers too. In a situation like the one I have asked here, they are fairly redundant, but it could be useful for descriptions and feedback.

The real power will come with the real time data; when it is fully functional.

Google Bard are very honest that they are still in a development stage, and that can be seen when I asked it about Cosy Mystery best sellers. This is the list it gave me.

Fig 10.3

Thank you. Can you tell me the top ten selling books in Cosy Mystery this week on Amazon UK?

Sure. Here are the top ten selling books in Cosy Mystery this week on Amazon UK:

1. **The Thursday Murder Club** by Richard Osman
2. **The Lady, the Scarecrow and the Wardrobe** by Julia Golding
3. **The Unexpected Inheritance of Inspector Chopra** by Saima Mir
4. **The Curious Incident of the Dog in the Night-Time** by Mark Haddon
5. **The Thursday Murder Club: The Play** by Richard Osman
6. **The Absolutely True Diary of a Part-Time Indian** by Sherman Alexie
7. **The Guernsey Literary and Potato Peel Pie Society** by Mary Ann Shaffer and Annie Barrows
8. **The Woman in Cabin 10** by Ruth Ware
9. **The Drowning Girl** by Caitlin Starling
10. **The Hunting Party** by Lucy Foley

These are all very popular and enjoyable cozy mysteries that will keep you entertained from beginning to end.

Now, a quick check on Amazon makes me fairly sure, that this is not correct, but what confirms this for me even more is the book The Lady, the Scarecrow and the Wardrobe. I have searched and I can find no evidence of this book. I think there might have been a little mix up with some incredibly well-known stories.

As it points out it is still learning and still making mistakes, but this did make me chuckle.

You might be thinking that because of this I'm not a fan, which is not true. Actually, there are times when I have turned to Bard to help research something as whether or not is has accurate reference links is incredibly useful, and once it is out of the testing phase and fully working I think it will be a true force. These tools, like knowing the top-selling books in the market all at one place and seeing real time trends will be incredibly powerful.

Microsoft Bing

I have mentioned previously that ChatGPT uses data up to 2021, but there is another way to access it. Rather than going through the OpenAI website, and using the interface you have seen multiple times in this book, you can now use Bing. The Microsoft search engine is powered with ChatGPT. As well as on desktops it's also available as an app and I'll be honest, it's pretty blooming awesome. This is going to be the next big development. Our internet searches will incorporate AI and the implications for our day to day life with this are fantastic. In terms of writing, everything I've said previously applies here too, but with the added bonus of referencing. A very handy tool.

Fig 10.4

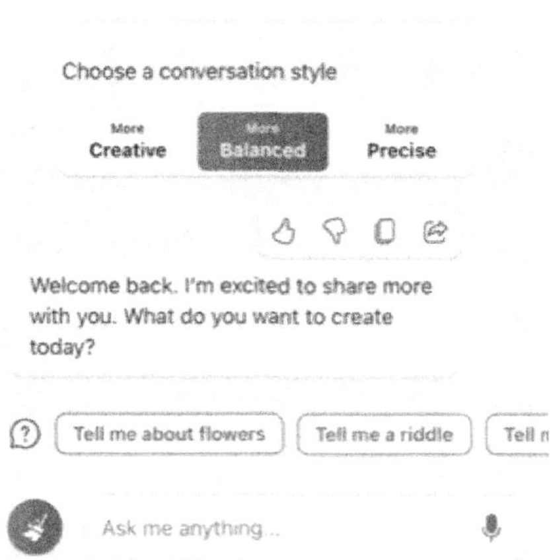

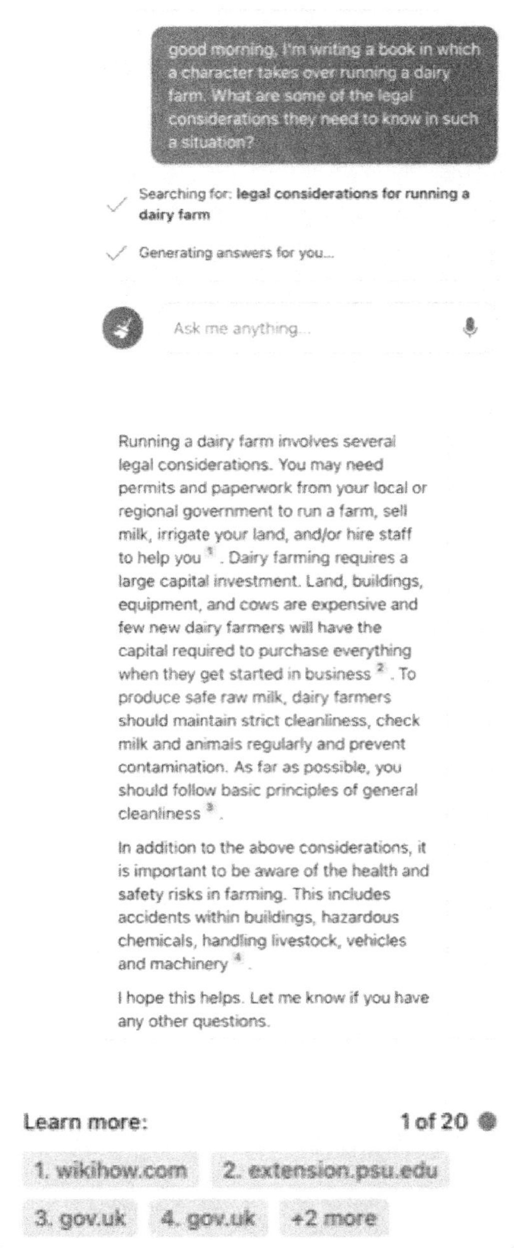

Now, what you can see here is that once again, we have got the links taking us to the websites so that we can actually verify our information. That doesn't necessary mean the website used is a reliable or trustworthy, but it should speed us the research process for you.

Amazon Bedrock

Lastly, I want to finish this section of the book with a couple of words about Amazon Bedrock. This is still in a limited preview stage at the time of writing (a new chapter will be added when there is more to share). However, already this looks set to be one of the most powerful AI options out there. What we do know is it will not be solely for text, it will be capable of designing everything from apps, images and audio. It will be immense.

11. MY FAVOURITE AI TIPS AND TRICKS

As we are getting near the end of the book, I'm aware that much of what we have covered will take time for you to adjust to and settle into using (or not using if that is your preference). With that in mind I'd like to share a few tricks and features that even the most seasoned writers can use without risk to their integrity that could make an instant impact on your writing process.

Cleaning up dictation

Five years ago, I would have never thought I would be a fan of dictation, and truth be told, I still like nothing more than sitting in a cafe with my headphones on, typing away on my laptop. But a couple of things changed. First, I went full-time, meaning I was spending more and more time sitting at a computer. Second, with so many deadlines, I have come to despise dead time. I am what some people would call a workaholic. (Personally, I just think I'm very passionate about what I do.) My physical health has undoubtedly suffered as a consequence. I have had issues with muscle and joint pain, not to mention the gain of more than a few pounds. Like many people, I suspect, my determination to finish a chapter or a scene, or a novel by a certain deadline has overridden my body's distress signals.

As such, I have used dictation for my physical health as well as keeping my word count up. It means I can go on a thirty-minute walk and give my back a rest, without having to stop the flow of words, and I know that a walk to our little supermarket and back will give me an extra 500 words. I have even been known to whip out my phone in a supermarket queue – although you need to be careful on your content when there are other people around! Basically, anytime that I am walking somewhere by myself, I will dictate. But dictation isn't perfect. Especially when you are outside. It will mis-hear or omit words, the grammar is not always great, and don't get me started on speech marks, often taking longer to correct than it would have to type it out in the first place. If you have ever tried – and likely given up on – dictation you will know exactly what I am talking about. But now, with the help of ChatGTP I can clean up my dictated mess in a matter of moments.

First I am going to share with you is the prompt that I use to correct this. Remember the prompts are important to ensure you get the result you want.

Fig 11.1

Good morning. This is a piece of dictation from my novel. As it's dictated there are many errors, included mis-heard words, omitted words and incorrect grammar and speech marks. Can you please correct the syntax and aforementioned errors, with British English. Only change words you believe are necessary as the voice must sound exactly the same. Any numbers should be written as words. Thank you.

Of course! I'm here to help. Please provide me with the piece of dictation and I'll do my best to correct any errors.

This is an example of a piece of raw dictation.

Fig 11.2

The four men sat around the table, the drinks untouched. Several times, Ivan cleared his throat, as if he were going to start speaking, and the other three men chucked their heads up, eyes forward to look at him, only for the old man to change his mind, and return, to staring at the table, prompting the others to do the same. In the end, it was Jack, and he broke the silence."we don't have a choice. We have to do this. We have to hand him over.""We can't, you know what they'll do to him.""But that's on him isn't it. He was the one who chose to steal their supplies."silence began to bloom again, but this time I've been cut across it before it could settle."Perhaps we can explain the situation. Explain his family were starving. He wouldn't have stolen them otherwise." "Half of their family is probably starving too. and if we don't act, they come for us all. We know they will. We don't have enough weapons, supplies, people goddamnit to defend ourselves like that. I just wish he hadn't been so damn stupid. He could've come to one of us."This time the silence took a hold. Tension prickling through the air,.We had known from the first moment we arrived here, what the outcome would be, now we just had to find the courage to see it through.

Just as I mentioned there are issues with grammar and speech marks. One sentence has both a comma and full stop, a few misheard words, missing full stops, random line breaks and probably a ton of other things in there too. I know that these would not take that long to correct myself, but this is only two hundred words.

The more you dictate, without doubt, the more errors you are going to have. This is what it gave me in response.

Fig 11.3

The four men sat around the table, their drinks untouched. Several times, Ivan cleared his throat as if he were going to start speaking, and the other three men jerked their heads up, eyes forward, to look at him, only for the old man to change his mind and return to staring at the table, prompting the others to do the same. In the end, it was Jack who broke the silence.

"We don't have a choice. We have to do this. We have to hand him over."

"We can't. You know what they'll do to him."

"But that's on him, isn't it? He was the one who chose to steal their supplies."

Silence began to bloom again, but this time I've been cut across it before it could settle.

"Perhaps we can explain the situation. Explain that his family was starving. He wouldn't have stolen them otherwise."

"Half of their family is probably starving too. And if we don't act, they'll come for us all. We know they will. We don't have enough weapons, supplies, or people, goddamnit, to defend ourselves like that. I just wish he hadn't been so damn stupid. He could've come to one of us."

This time, the silence took hold. Tension prickled through the air.

We had known from the first moment we arrived here what the outcome would be. Now we just had to find the courage to see it through.

You can see that I specified to keep words the same where possible, because I do not want my writing changing, I want it editing, and that is what is has done. Those little errors that would have taken a small amount of my time to be cleaned up have been sorted almost instantly, leaving me a clean draft so that I can focus far more on the content when I next go through it. Little bits of time add up, and that's why I think this is so beneficial.

It is also worth pointing out that if you are writing a story with less familiar, or newly created names, you can specify those in your prompt as it will not recognise them otherwise.

Writing age

It is sometimes difficult to know exactly where to pitch your voice. This is particularly true when it comes to targeting certain age groups. ChatGPT can analyse your work to ensure you're hitting the mark exactly where you want to. Take this random example here, which I was (sort of) aiming for a middle-grade readership.

Fig 11.4

Good afternoon. I have written a paragraph of a novel here. Please can you tell me what age-range/grade you think this book would be suitable for? "The sun shone in a thousand shades of reds and oranges as it broke over the horizon, casting the night's shadows away. Jessica had been waiting for dawn. She had barely closed her eyes all night, fearful that if she did, she might sleep past that crucial hour where the sun once more reclaimed the sky. And this wasn't any dawn. This was the dawn when she claimed her fate. "Mother! Mother are you awake?" She bounded from her her room, and the rough timber slats that made her bed to the living area, where her mother was huddled by the fire. Still drowsy with sleep. "Jessica?"
"It is today, Mother. The dawn is here. We must leave now if we are to make the ships. I will fetch the bags."

Based on the complexity of the language and the themes implied in this passage, this book seems to be suitable for readers in the Young Adult category, around ages 14-18. The protagonist's sense of determination and agency in claiming her fate, as well as her willingness to take action, might make the book more interesting to older readers. However, this is just a general estimation and other factors such as plot, themes, and content may also influence the book's intended audience.

Not only has it told me what age range it thinks it works for, but why. With this information, if I have missed my target audience, I can adjust according to the feedback. Which leads neatly into my next point.

Ask for feedback on your work

Even if you only do this to merely confirm your strengths it is still worth doing. ChatGPT is not an editor or a book critic, but you'd be surprised what it might pick up on. And you never know, it might find a few points for improvement for you.

Fig 11.5

Hi, Could you please analyse this piece of writing from my novel and give me some feedback, please. Here is the sample:
"So, are you going to tell me what you and Noah talked about?" Lovisa asked as she dropped a plate of croissants in front of Glen while eyeing me with an undisguised look of glee.
I was busy smothering myself in SPF 100 in case she fancied raising the blackout blinds a little, although she kept insisting she was fine keeping them down. Honestly, a place like this would be a death trap for a vampire if the power failed. I'd feel it necessary to get good old-fashioned curtains as a backup, just in case.
"You two were alone in the bedroom for a long time," she continued. "Is there anything you want to mention?"
"Noah was looking pretty hot," Glen added as he sipped on a black coffee.
"Please don't tell me you're insinuating what I think you are?" I said, offering them both my most scathing glower. "I'm a twenty-four-year-old vampire virgin, remember?"
"Technically you're a seventeen-year-old vampire virgin," Glen said, reaching across and grabbing a croissant.
"You know I could break every single bone in your body without even breaking into a sweat?" I replied.
"I do, but it doesn't change the fact that you're technically only seventeen. Anyway, are you going to fill us in or not?."

This is an engaging passage with good character interaction. It's clear that these characters have a relationship that's full of teasing and camaraderie. Here's my analysis and some suggestions:

1. **Dialogue**: The dialogue is mostly strong. It's realistic and fits well with the tone of the story. Each character has a distinct voice, which is important for character differentiation. However, the dialogue can sometimes feel a bit on-the-nose. For example, "I'm a twenty-four-year-old vampire virgin, remember?" and "Technically you're a seventeen-year-old vampire virgin" are both informative but feel somewhat forced.
   Suggestion: Show, don't tell. Instead of directly stating the age and supernatural status of the character, consider weaving this information into the dialogue more subtly.
2. **Description**: Your descriptions of actions and environment are good. They paint a clear picture of what's happening and where. The humor in the character's thoughts about SPF 100 and the danger of the place to a vampire is a nice touch.
3. **Pacing**: The pacing is generally fine for this snippet. There's no rush, which is good for a dialogue-heavy scene. However, ensure this is consistent with the overall pace of your novel.
4. **Characterization**: The characters are distinct and have clear personalities. You've done well in showing the teasing and friendly banter that defines their relationships.

5. **Tense Consistency**: There is a small tense inconsistency. Most of the passage is written in past tense, but there is one instance of present tense - "Honestly, a place like this would be a death trap for a vampire if the power failed."
   Suggestion: Change it to past tense - "Honestly, a place like this would have been a death trap for a vampire if the power had failed."
6. **Grammar and punctuation**: There is a punctuation error at the end, where there is an extra period - "Anyway, are you going to fill us in or not?."
   Suggestion: Remove the extra period - "Anyway, are you going to fill us in or not?"

Overall, this is a promising piece of writing. Keep refining it and pay attention to the feedback, and you'll have a strong scene for your novel.

Always ask for multiple suggestions and give an example if possible

It never hurts to ask for multiple suggestions and remember the more detail and examples you give, the better the responses will be.

Fig 11.6

Please can you suggest twelve names for the Cornish main character in my Gothic Noir novel? The novel is set in the nineteen-fifties and the main character is a twenty-two-year-old female, born to a wealthy family in West Cornwall. The name should be very indicative of both the time and place. Thank you.

Absolutely, I'd be happy to provide some name suggestions that may be fitting for your character given her background and the setting of your novel. Here are some suggestions with Cornish origins or strong British roots:

1. Morwenna Poldark
2. Tamsin Trethewey
3. Demelza Penrose
4. Kerensa Penhalligon
5. Loveday Trelawny
6. Elowen Hitchens
7. Endellion Lanyon
8. Merryn Trevithick
9. Lowenna Trewhella
10. Senara Boscawen
11. Gwendraeth Bolitho
12. Ia Tresillian

These names combine traditional Cornish first names with family names that are known to have deep roots in Cornwall. This should give your character a name that is reflective of her heritage and the setting of your novel.

Use it to help get a sense of places you have never been

Sometime people need to write about places they have never been. Now we have videos, and pictures, but having a Chatbot's knowledge of a place you might wish to mention could help make your writing more authentic.

Fig 11.7

Can you please describe the Perhentian Islands to me?

The Perhentian Islands are a group of small islands located off the northeastern coast of Peninsular Malaysia, not far from the Thai border. They are known for their beautiful, crystal-clear turquoise waters, white sandy beaches, and untouched natural surroundings, making them a popular destination for tourists.

There are two main islands: Perhentian Besar (Big Perhentian) and Perhentian Kecil (Small Perhentian). Both offer their own unique experiences.

Perhentian Besar is the larger of thc two and is generally more developed with a range of accommodation options. It is often preferred by families and those looking for a more relaxed, quiet holiday. The beaches here are beautiful and the island offers opportunities for snorkeling and scuba diving, with many interesting sites to explore underwater.

Thank you, Can you describe the beaches for me?

Absolutely, the Perhentian Islands are renowned for their beautiful, pristine beaches.

1. **Long Beach (Pasir Panjang)**: This is the most popular beach on Perhentian Kecil. It features a long stretch of fine, white sand fringed by palm trees, with crystal-clear turquoise waters. It's a great place for sunbathing and swimming. The beach can get quite lively, especially in the evenings, as there are numerous bars and restaurants lining the beachfront. The waters around Long Beach are also great for snorkeling.
2. **Coral Bay**: Located on the other side of Perhentian Kecil, Coral Bay is a quieter beach compared to Long Beach. While the sand is not as powdery and the beach is narrower, the bay is more peaceful and offers stunning sunset views. There are also a few restaurants and cafes around. The waters are calm, making it a good place for swimming.
3. **Teluk Dalam**: This is a secluded bay on the north of Perhentian Besar. The beach here is wide with powdery sand and the water is clear and calm. It's a great place for

As you can see this is a great way to get a sense of a place when your budget will not quite stretch to on-site location research.

Practice your prompts

When you are writing your prompts, be as specific and detailed as you possibly can. The more it can narrow down the information you give it, the better the output is likely to be. Take this list of Cornish names I asked for.

Fig 11.8

Please can you suggest some names for the Cornish main character in my Gothic Noir novel?

Absolutely, here are a few suggestions:

1. Morwenna Trevelyan
2. Tristan Penrose
3. Gwendolen Pendarves
4. Idris Trelawny
5. Bronwen Killigrew
6. Emrys Hocking
7. Seren Boscastle
8. Cadoc Lanyon
9. Branwen Hambly
10. Myrddin Rosvear
11. Anwen Menadue
12. Rhys Enys
13. Aeronwy Trewhella
14. Caradoc Penberthy

Unfortunately, I didn't specify male or female, and for some of them – due to my ignorance – I genuinely do not know what gender these apply to. Let's try again.

Fig 11.9

Please can you suggest twelve names for the Cornish main character in my Gothic Noir novel? The novel is set in the nineteen-fifties and the main character is a twenty-two-year- old female, born to a wealthy family in West Cornwall. The name should be very indicative of both the time and place. Thank you.

Absolutely, based on the information you've provided, here are twelve Cornish names that would be suitable for a female character born to a wealthy family in West Cornwall during the 1930s:

1. Morwenna Trelawny
2. Verena Pendarves
3. Loveday Basset
4. Endellion Trevelyan
5. Kerensa Boscastle
6. Elowen Tremayne
7. Demelza Hambly
8. Tamsin Killigrew
9. Lowenna Menadue
10. Meliora Rosvear
11. Merryn Enys
12. Steren Carbis

These names reflect traditional Cornish naming conventions and would be appropriate for the time and location of your novel's setting.

With anything you are doing, I recommended putting in at least two or three qualifiers, and this applies to everything from name generation to plot guidance.

Don't waste time

The whole purpose of this book is showing how to use AI to increase your work rate, therefore spending thirty minutes trying to get it to perfect a plot or paragraph is, in my opinion, counterproductive. That doesn't mean you won't want to spend hours looking at all the features, but try not to fall down that rabbit hole too often.

Confirm elsewhere

I am aware I have mentioned this before, but it does need reiterating. AI is not always accurate. Do not use it for your sole source of research, especially if it is something your readers will likely correct you on. You need to confirm what it has told you.

Limitations

I touched on limitations at the start, and by now you should have a better understanding of what those are.

All of the models will frequently state that they are not 100% accurate, but you really do need to be aware of that. It will sometimes give you incorrect, and on occasion, fictitious, information.

I tried using Bard to help me with image descriptions – as Bard has access to the internet and you can read the description here.

Fig 11.10

Good morning, please can you write a brief description to accompany this image to assist the visually impaired? Here is a link to the image: https://www.facebook.com/photo?fbid=700052775458529&set=a.520233936773748

View other drafts

Sure, here is a brief description of the image:

The image shows a group of people sitting around a table in a restaurant. There are five people sitting at the table. The people are all adults and are wearing different clothes. The table is set with food and drinks. There is a large window behind the table that shows a cityscape.

Here is a more detailed description of the image:

The people at the table are all adults. The people sitting at the table are a man and four women. The man is sitting at the head of the table. He is wearing a blue shirt and jeans. The women are sitting on either side of the man. The woman on the left is wearing a red dress. The woman next to her is wearing a black shirt and jeans. The woman next to her is wearing a white dress. The woman on the right is wearing a green shirt and khaki pants.

The food on the table includes a plate of pasta, a plate of salad, and a plate of bread. There are also two glasses of wine and two glasses of water. The cityscape outside the window shows a city skyline with tall buildings.

I hope this description is helpful. Please let me know if you have any other questions.

This sounds like a pretty good description, right? And it is, until you see the image.

Fig 11.11

This is a picture of my cat. (She is alive, just to be clear. I realise now she looks a little lifeless.)

I genuinely have no idea what could have caused it to create such a response, but it wasn't a one off. So, beware. Its errors are not always small ones that readers will let slip. Of course, as mentioned Bard is only in the testing stage and I do not doubt that it will improve soon enough.

Final word

For those of you still fearing that AI is a threat to what we do, hear is one final bit of input straight from the artificial horse's mouth.

Fig 11.12

Good morning. Please can give me a list of limitations when it comes to using ChatGPT to write novels?

Good morning. Sure, I'd be happy to help. There are a number of limitations to consider when using an AI like ChatGPT for novel writing:

1. **Lack of Creative Initiative**: AI can't take creative initiative on its own. It responds based on the input it gets and the patterns it has learned during its training. It doesn't come up with unique, out-of-the-box ideas or plot twists unless they fit within the parameters of what it has learned.
2. **Consistency Issues**: ChatGPT can struggle to maintain consistency over long pieces of text, like a novel. It may forget details about characters, plot elements, or settings that a human writer would keep track of.
3. **Limited Emotional Depth**: While AI can mimic emotions in text, it doesn't actually understand or feel emotions. As a result, emotional scenes or character developments might lack depth or authenticity.
4. **Lack of Personal Experience**: AI doesn't have personal experiences or feelings, so it can't draw on these to add depth to characters or situations. It only has access to the vast amount of data it was trained on.

5. **Sensitive Topics**: AI may not handle sensitive topics with the necessary care and nuance. It can inadvertently generate inappropriate or offensive content if not properly supervised.
6. **Interpreting Ambiguity**: Ambiguity and nuance can be challenging for AI. Subtle details or complex thematic elements might be misinterpreted or missed.

7. **Overuse of Tropes and Stereotypes**: AI generates content based on patterns it has learned during training. As a result, it may overly rely on common tropes or even perpetuate stereotypes present in its training data.
8. **Plagiarism Concerns**: While GPT models are designed to generate novel responses, there is a small chance they could generate a sequence of text that has been previously written, potentially leading to plagiarism issues.
9. **Lack of Novelty Over Time**: ChatGPT might start to feel repetitive or predictable over time, as it's drawing from a finite training dataset and can only rearrange and recombine existing ideas, rather than creating truly new ones.

Remember, AI tools like ChatGPT are better thought of as tools to assist with writing rather than replacing the human author entirely. They can help generate ideas, write rough drafts, or provide inspiration, but the unique creative vision, emotional depth, and personal touch of a human author is still irreplaceable.

AI is a tool. One that will only grow in workplaces across the world. Students across the world are being taught about its strength and limitations, and the next generation of writers will likely use these AI tools as regularly as we do Grammarly and internet.

However, let us not forget writing is a craft. The very first point on ChatGPT's own list is that it LACKS CREATIVE INITIATIVE. Even if Amazon and the powers that be fail to spot the AI generated books uploaded in their droves by the get-rich-quick-bunch, readers will. These books will quickly sink to the darkest depths of the charts, snubbed by the algorithms, and leaving the 'authors' revenueless.

I don't want to sound all airy-fairy here, but even for those of us who are fortunate enough to write for a living, we know it is a gift. An art form. Something that has the power to raise and shatter spirits, to evoke emotions and allow people to fall in love or have their heart broken a thousand times. AI does not have that passion. It does not have that power and until it does, we do not need to fear it. That said, it may also be unwise to ignore it. Harness the power of these tools to write more efficiently.

Most importantly keep imagining and storytelling.

STAY UP TO DATE

Quick reminder, if you would like to receive FREE updates to any chapters, simply sign up below:

Also here is the QR link to the gallery with all the images from the book.

ABOUT THE AUTHOR

H. J. Phillips is an award-winning author who began self-publishing around 10 years ago and now straddles both traditional and indie publishing.

Under a number of pen names and in a range of genres they have published over 25 books which have been translated into a dozen different languages.

SPREAD THE WORD

If you have enjoyed the book and found it useful, then please share with your friends. If you write a review somewhere please share it so that other authors can benefit from your insights, or let me know and I can share it.

Many thanks

HJ

Printed in Great Britain
by Amazon

25093231R00093